Political Theology

972-839-1500

April 17- Kasey 617-504-4545

March 31-2 Karen 212-608-8690

Political Theology

Four Chapters on the
Concept of Sovereignty

Carl Schmitt

Translated by George Schwab
Foreword by Tracy B. Strong

The University of Chicago Press
Chicago and London

The University of Chicago Press, Chicago 60637

This translation © 1985 by George Schwab

This book was originally published as *Politische Theologie: Vier Kapitel zur Lehre von der Souveranitat* © 1922, revised edition © 1934 by Duncker & Humblot, Berlin.

This translation first published in the United States by MIT Press, in the series Studies in Contemporary German Social Thought, edited by Thomas McCarthy.

Foreword © 2005 by Tracy B. Strong

University of Chicago Press edition 2005

Printed in the United States of America

10 09 08   4 5

ISBN: 0-226-73889-2

Library of Congress Cataloging-in-Publication Data

Schmitt, Carl, 1888–

    [Politische Theologie. English]

    Political theology : four chapters on the concept of sovereignty / Carl Schmitt ; translated by George Schwab ; foreword by Tracy Strong.—University of Chicago Press ed.

      p. cm.

    Translation of Politische Theologie.

    Originally published: Cambridge, Mass. : MIT Press, c1985 in series: Studies in contemporary German social thought.

    Includes bibliographical references and index.

    ISBN 0-226-73889-2

    1. Sovereignty. 2. Political theology. I. Title.

JC327 .S3813 2005

320.1′5—dc22

2005048576

Contents

3 Political Theology

Theological conceptions in the theory of the state. The sociology of juristic concepts, especially of the concept of sovereignty. The correspondence between the social structure of an epoch and its metaphysical view of the world, especially between the monarchical state and the theistic world view. The transition from conceptions of transcendence to those of immanence from the eighteenth to the nineteenth century (democracy, the organic theory of the state, the identity of law and the state).

4 On the Counterrevolutionary Philosophy of the State (de Maistre, Bonald, Donoso Cortés)

Decisionism in the counterrevolutionary philosophy of the state. Authoritarian and anarchist theories based on the opposing theses of the "naturally evil" and "naturally good" human being. The position of the liberal bourgeoisie and Donoso Cortés's definition of it. The development from legitimacy to dictatorship in the history of ideas.

Index

Foreword

The Sovereign and the Exception: Carl Schmitt, Politics, Theology, and Leadership

In memory and appreciation of Wilson Carey McWilliams, 1933–2005

He who fights with monsters should look to it that he himself does not become a monster. And when you gaze long into an abyss the abyss also gazes into you.
                              Nietzsche, *Beyond Good and Evil*

Political Theology is about the nature, and thus about the prerogatives, of sovereign political authority as it develops in the West, about its relation to Western Christianity, and about some of its foremost exponents. While by no means the first writing of Carl Schmitt, it is perhaps the piece that best serves as an introduction to his thought.

Schmitt was a—perhaps *the*—leading jurist during the Weimar Republic. In May 1933, he joined the National Socialist German Workers Party (the Nazi Party), the same month as did Martin Heidegger, the leading philosopher in Germany. In November of that year he became the president of the National Socialist Jurists Association. He published several works that were supportive of the Nazi Party, including some that were anti-

1. G. Balakrishnan, *The Enemy: An Intellectual Portrait of Carl Schmitt* (London: Verso, 2000). Balakrishnan argues that until the last years of the Weimar Republic Schmitt expressed no anti-Semitic views and that during the Nazi period, he "became skilled at transforming crude anti-Semitic ideograms into a higher order theoretical discourse." See also the exchange between him and Scheuerman, "Down on Law: The complicated legacy of the authoritarian jurist Carl Schmitt" in *Boston Review* (April–May 2001).

Semitic.[1] All did not go smoothly: one tends to forget that there were diverse factions in Nazism, as there are in all political movements, and Schmitt found himself on the losing side of several controversies. Criticized in several official organs, he was protected by Hermann Goering. He remained a member of the Party as well as professor of law at the University of Berlin between 1933 and 1945, and was detained afterwards by the victorious Allies, but never charged with crimes. He died in April 1985.[2]

As early as 1938 and again after World War II, Schmitt was fond of recalling *Benito Cereno*, one of Herman Melville's novels, in obvious reference to his choices in 1933 and after.[3] The novel was translated into German in 1939 and was apparently widely read and discussed in terms of the contemporary political situation.[4] The title character in *Benito Cereno* is the captain of a slave ship that has been taken over by the African slaves. The owner of the slaves and most of the white crew have been killed, although Don Benito is left alive and forced by the slaves' leader, Babo, to play the role of captain so as not to arouse suspicion from other ships. Eventually, after a prolonged encounter with the frigate of the American Captain Delano during which the American at first

---

2. See the discussion in my "Dimensions of the Debate Around Carl Schmitt," Foreword to Carl Schmitt, *The Concept of the Political* (Chicago: University of Chicago Press, 1996), x–xii, and the references cited there for further discussion of these events.

3. Carl Schmitt, *Ex Captivitate Salus: Erfahrungen der Zeit 1945/47* (Cologne: Greven Verlag, 1950), 22–77. Thanks to John McCormick for this reference. Let me take this occasion to pay tribute to McCormick's wonderful book on Carl Schmitt, *Carl Schmitt's Critique of Liberalism: Against Politics as Technology* (Cambridge: Cambridge University Press, 1997), from which I have learned a great deal.

4. Schmitt notes that "Benito Cereno, the hero [!!] of Herman Melville's story, was elevated in Germany to the level of a symbol for the situation of persons of intelligence caught in a mass system." Schmitt, "Remarks in response to a talk by Karl Mannheim (1945–1946)," in *Ex Captivate Salus. Expériences des années 1945–1947. Textes et commentaires*, ed. A. Doremus (Paris: Vrin, 2003), 133.

suspects Cereno of malfeasance—he cannot conceive of the possibility that slaves have taken over a ship—the truth comes out: the slaves are recaptured and imprisoned, some executed.

In a letter apparently written on his fiftieth birthday in 1938, Schmitt signed himself as "Benito Cereno."[5] This passage from the end of the novel, although not one I know Schmitt to have cited explicitly, is in particular relevant:

"Only at the end did my suspicions [of you, said Captain Delano to Benito Cereno] get the better of me, and you know how wide of the mark they then proved."

"Wide, indeed," said Don Benito, sadly; "you were with me all day; stood with me, sat with me, talked with me, looked at me, ate with me, drank with me; and yet, your last act was to clutch for a villain, not only an innocent man, but the most pitiable of all men. To such degree may malign machinations and deceptions impose. So far may even the best men err, in judging the conduct of one with the recesses of whose condition he is not acquainted. But you were forced to it; and you were in time undeceived. Would that, in both respects, it was so ever, and with all men."

"I think I understand you; you generalize, Don Benito; and mournfully enough. But the past is passed; why moralize upon it? Forget it. See, yon bright sun has forgotten it all, and the blue sea, and the blue sky; these have turned over new leaves."[6]

5. Copies of the supposed letter were sent to several people after the War, among them Arnim Mohler, who reprinted it in the publication of his correspondence with Schmitt. (Mohler was the historian-theorist of the "conservative revolution" in Germany, and, as director of the Carl Siemens-Stiftung after the war, a central intellectual figure of the extreme right in Germany.) Schmitt had apparently wanted this letter to become the epigraph to a reissuing of his book on Hobbes, *Der Leviathan in der Staatslehre des Thomas Hobbes. Sinn und Feldschlag eines politischen Symbols* (Hamburg: Hanseatische Verlaganstalt, 1938), which could then be taken as an esoteric text of resistance to Nazism. Wolfgang Palaver ("Carl Schmitt, mythologue politique," in Carl Schmitt, *Le Léviathan dans la doctrine de l'état de Thomas Hobbes* [Paris: Seuil, 2002], 220–24) casts considerable doubt on the complete (though not the partial) truth of this possibility. See also Carl Schmitt, *Ex Captivate Salus. Experiences des années 1945–1947. Textes et commentaires*, ed. A. Doremus (Paris: Vrin, 2003), 209.

6. Hermann Melville, *Benito Cereno* in Herman Melville, *Billy Budd and Other Tales* (New York: The New American Library, 1961).

How was it, the captain of the second ship wishes to know, that Benito Cereno was taken in by the evil brewing under his nose? Cereno notes that had he been more acute, it might in fact have cost him his life. Indeed, as he protests, since "malign machinations and deceptions impose" themselves on all human beings, he had no choice but to play the role in which Babo had cast him. That Schmitt was fond of calling upon the Melville story is complexly revelatory. The captain of a ship might be thought of as the model of what we mean by a "sovereign." Yet here we have a story about a man obliged to accept the pose of being in control while actually going along with evil because his safety required it. At the very end of Melville's story, after Babo and the other slaves have been captured, a shroud falls from the bowsprit of Cereno's erstwhile ship to reveal the skeleton of the slave owner murdered by the revolted slaves, and over it the inscription "Follow your leader." *Benito Cereno* is about, among other things, what being a sovereign or captain is, how one is to recognize one, and the mistakes that can be made when one doesn't.[7]

The present volume, reissued with a new foreword but otherwise "unchanged" in a second edition in November 1933, after Schmitt had joined the Nazi party, can thus be read on one hand as a document relevant to Schmitt's decision to see himself as allied with the NSDAP, and what that allegiance meant. To see the choice that Schmitt (or Heidegger, or many other German philosophers, theologians, artists, as well as people from all walks of life—not just in Germany, and not just then) made as blind or

---

7. William Scheuerman (*The End of Law* [Lanham: Rowman and Littlefield: 1999], 176–78) advances an alternate reading to the effect that Schmitt's invocation of *Benito Cereno* is designed not so much to exculpate himself from the worst of the Nazi taint but to evince his distress at being subject to the multi-racial, Jew-dominated American occupying power. It is possible that this is true postwar but, assuming that Schmitt actually did write the letter in 1938, hardly could have been true beforehand. These understandings are not mutually exclusive.

ignorant or born from venal ambition, is, I think, to misunderstand their thought and their life. It is also to sweep under the table what appeared as the appeal and apparent necessity of such a movement, and to avoid serious engagement with why it appeared as such.

* * *

The above is written as preliminary. Schmitt also appears to us as the author of some of the most searching works of political theory in the last century, books whose appeal has over time covered the political spectrum from Left to Right. What is the nature of his importance and his appeal? The present volume is also a central document in answer to that question.

Political Theology was originally published in 1922 and it represents Schmitt's most important initial engagement with the theme that was to preoccupy him for most of his life: that of sovereignty—that is, of the locus and nature of the agency that constitutes a political system. The first sentence of *Political Theology* is famous: it locates the realm in which Schmitt asserts the question of the centrality of sovereignty. Schmitt places the sentence as the complete initial paragraph in the body of the book. He writes: "Sovereign is he who decides on the exceptional case."[8]

Translation is always interpretation, and the opening sentence raises immediately a number of issues. The first is consequent to the nature and range of the "decide." The German is *"Soverän ist, wer über den Ausnahmezustand entscheidet."*[9] The decisive matter comes from the fact that translation imposes on us the temptation to think that *über* is ambiguous: in English the sentence can be rendered "he who decides *what* the exceptional case is" or "he who

8. Carl Schmitt, *Political Theology* (Cambridge, Mass.: MIT Press, 1985), 5 (hereafter cited in text as *PT*).
9. Carl Schmitt, *Politisches Theologie* (Berlin: Duncker und Humblot, [2002] 2004).

decides *what to do* about the exceptional case."[10] George Schwab's fine translation in this volume—"decides on the exception"—retains the ambiguity, if it condenses "case" into "exception." Yet the fact that this may appear ambiguous in English or German should not detain us in a misguided manner: retaining the seeming ambiguity is central to grasping what Schmitt wants to say. We can see this in part in the fact that e*ntscheiden über* can also mean "to settle on": Schmitt is saying that it is the essence of sovereignty *both* to decide what is an exception *and* to make the decisions appropriate to that exception, indeed that one without the other makes no sense at all.

It is thus not only the case that "exceptions" are obvious, as they would be if we think of them as when produced by severe economic or political disturbance. It could appear natural to read what Schmitt says in Germany back through the years of hyperinflation or the economic depression of 1929. *Political Theology*, however, was published in March 1922 and cannot be understood as simply the response to these or any other developments (hyper-

---

10. This is noted also by John McCormick in "The Dilemmas of Dictatorship: Carl Schmitt and Constitutional Emergency Powers," in D. Dyzenhaus, ed., *Law as Politics: Carl Schmitt's Critique of Liberalism* (Durham, N.C.: Duke University Press, 1998), 223. McCormick sees this, too strongly for me, as a move by Schmitt away from conservatism towards fascism (218). See my discussion of Schmitt's doctrine of sovereignty immediately below. For the problem in French, see the discussion by Julien Freund, a friend of Schmitt and a contributor to his Festschrift, in the right-wing French journal *La nouvelle école*, 44 (Spring 1987): 17. Freund opts in French for *lors* (during, on the occasion of) as the translation of *über*. This judgment is refused by Jean-Louis Schlegel, the editor of the Gallimard French edition of *Théologie politique* (Gallimard: Paris, 1988), 15, who gives *décide de*. See my discussion of right-wing, left-wing, and liberal uses and misuses of Schmitt in "Dimensions of the New Debate Around Carl Schmitt," Introduction to Carl Schmitt, *The Concept of the Political* (Chicago: University of Chicago Press, 1996). For a recent defense of Schmitt by the French Right, see Alain de Benoist, "Carl Schmitt et les sagouins [a sagouin is a slob or slovenly person]," *Eléments* n°110, septembre 2003, available online at http://www.grece-fr.net/textes/_txtWeb.php?idArt=180.

inflation hits only in 1923). Indeed, George Schwab's careful re-
construction of Schmitt's analysis of Article 48 of the Weimar
constitution (xix–xxi, this volume) shows that Schmitt had a very
broad interpretation of what the President might do if "public security and order [were] considerably disturbed . . ."[11]

A second translation issue with the opening sentence unfolds
from the understanding of *Ausnahmezustand*. What the first translation might seem to reinforce (the absolute and dictatorial and
unlimited quality of the decision), this second one might seem to
mitigate. A dictionary will tell you that the word means "state of
emergency." The idea of a "state of emergency," however, has
more of a legal connotation, and is more confined than an "exception." It is also the case, as Jean-Louis Schlegel points out, that
Schmitt sometimes uses more general words when speaking of
"the exception," including "state of exception" (*Ausnahmefall*),
"crisis or state of urgency" (*Notstand*), and even more generally
"emergency, state of need" (*Notfall*).[12] Thus the same issue is
raised as with the *über*: can the understanding of what counts as
an "exception" be defined in legal terms, or is it more of what one
might think of as an open field?[13]

Note here that Schmitt is not talking simply about dictatorship.
In *Die Diktatur*, published one year before PT, Schmitt differ-
entiates between "commissarial dictatorship"—he cites Lincoln

11. See the fine discussion in J. P. McCormick, "The Dilemmas of Dictatorship: Carl
Schmitt and Constitutional Emergency Powers," in Dyzenhaus, *Law as Politics*, 217–51.

12. Schlegel, *Théologie politique*, 15n.

13. One should note here that this question bedevils all situations in which constitutions provide for an exception. For a brief history of nineteenth- and twentieth-century constitutional
provisions for exception, including the French 1814 Constitution, World War One in France
and Switzerland, the 1920 Emergency Powers Act in England, Lincoln at the beginning of
the Civil War (noted by Schmitt in *Die Diktatur* [Munich: Duncker und Humblot, 1921],
136), the United States under Wilson during World War One, Article 16 of the French Fifth
Republic, etc., see Giorgio Agamben, *State of Exception* (Chicago: University of Chicago
Press, 2005), 11–26.

in the Civil war as an example—and "sovereign dictatorship." The former defends the existing constitution and the latter seeks to create the conditions for a new one, given the collapse of the old—one might think to some degree of de Gaulle in 1958. *Die Dikatur* is a theory of dictatorship; *PT*, however, is a theory of sovereignty and an attempt to locate the state of emergency in a theory of sovereignty. More importantly, *PT* in effect discusses that which for Schmitt lies under the various kinds of dictatorship and makes both of them possible.[14]

I again do not think this linguistic glide on Schmitt's part to be accidental. Rather than seeking to determine what precisely an "exception" (or an "emergency" or a "crisis," etc.) is, the problem should be looked at from the other direction. It is importantly the case for Schmitt that no pre-existing set of rules can be laid down to make explicit whether this situation "is" in actual reality an "exception." It is of the essence of Schmitt's conception of the state that there can be no preset rule-fixed definition of sovereignty.[15] Why not? What is clear here is that the notion of sovereignty contains, as Schmitt tells us, his general theory of the state (*PT*, 5). The nature of the sovereign, he remarks in the preface to the second edition (1934), is the making of a "genuine decision" (*PT*, 3). Thus it is not simply the making of a decision, but of a "genuine" decision that is central. The obvious question is what makes a decision "genuine" and not simply an emanation of a "degenerate decisionism." Schmitt is never "simply" a decision-

---

14. I thus resist John McCormick's conclusion that *PT* "repudiates much of what is of value in the book published before it" in his "Dilemmas of Dictatorship," in Dyzenhaus, *Law as Politics*, 241.

15. Thus the exception is part of the "order" even if that order is not precisely juridical. Schmitt engaged in an exchange about this with Walter Benjamin over violence. See Benjamin, "Towards a Critique of Violence," in Walter Benjamin, *Selected Writings*, vol. 1 (Cambridge: Harvard University Press, 1996). See the discussion in Agamben, *State of Exception*, 52–64.

ist, if by that one means simply that choice is necessary and any choice is better than none.[16]

What constitutes a "genuine decision" is a complex matter in Schmitt. To understand his position one must realize why politics (or here, "the political") is not the same for Schmitt as "the state,"[17] even if the most usual framework for the concretization of politics in modern times has been the state.[18] In a book published in 1969 that takes up the themes of *PT*, Schmitt writes "today one can no longer define politics in terms of the State; on the contrary what we can still call the State today must inversely be defined and understood from the political."[19] Underlying the state is a community of people—necessarily not universal—a "we" that, as it defines itself necessarily in opposition to that which it is not, presupposes and is defined by conflict.[20] It derives its definition from the friend/enemy distinction. That distinction, however, is an us/them distinction, in which the "us" is of primary and necessary importance.

16. I note here that there seem to be strong elements of Schmitt quietly present in much of Henry Kissinger's analyses of international politics. See for instance his *The Necessity for Choice* (New York: Harper, 1961).

17. This is a theme from Schmitt's earliest work, including his *Habilitationsschrift, Der Wert des Staates und die Bedeutung des Einzeln* (Tübingen: Hellerau, 1917). See Reinhard Mehring, *Carl Schmitt. Zur Einführung* (Hamburg: Junius, 2001), 19–21.

18. Cf. Max Weber's definition of the state: "Nowadays, however, we have to say that the state is the form of human community that (successfully) lays claim to the monopoly of legitimate violence within a given territory . . ." Max Weber, "Politics as a Vocation," in *The Vocation Lectures*, ed. David Owen and Tracy B. Strong, 33 (Hackett, 2002). See the discussion of this passage in our introduction to the Weber lectures, xlix. It is important that this is the definition to which the "nowadays" compels us and that Weber here flies directly in the face of those (like the Georgkreis and others) who placed emphasis on the "nation," on "blood and soil."

19. Carl Schmitt, *Politisches Theologie II* (Berlin: Duncker und Humblot, [1969] 1996), 21.

20. One thus finds the influence of Schmitt for instance in what might appear to be a far removed locus, e.g. Bertram de Jouvenel, *The Pure Theory of Politics* (New Haven, Conn.: Yale University Press, 1964).

This claim is at the basis of Schmitt's rejection of what he calls "liberal normativism"—that is, of the assumption that a state can ultimately rest on a set of mutually agreed-to procedures and rules that trump particular claims and necessities. Pluralism is thus not a condition on which politics, and therefore eventually the state, can be founded. Politics rests rather on the equality of its citizens (in this sense Schmitt is a "democrat") and thus their collective differentiation from other such groups: this is the "friend/enemy" distinction, or more accurately the distinction that makes politics possible. It is, one might say, its transcendental presupposition.[21]

Politics is thus different from economics, where one has "competitors" rather than friends and enemies, as it is different from debate, where one has *Diskussionsgegner* (discussion opponents).[22] It is not a private dislike of another individual; rather it is the actual possibility of a "battling totality" (*kämpfende Gesamtheit*) that finds itself necessarily in opposition to another such entity. "The enemy," Schmitt notes, "is *hostis* (enemy) not *inimicus* (disliked) in the broader sense; *polémios* (belonging to war) not *exthrós* (hateful)."[23]

These considerations are made in the context of several other

21. This is confirmed explicitly in a letter from Leo Strauss to Schmitt, September 4, 1932. It is printed in *Heinrich Meier, Carl Schmitt, and Leo Strauss: The Hidden Dialogue* (Chicago: University of Chicago Press, 1995), 124. Meier's book is an insightful analysis of the difference between political theology and political philosophy—between Schmitt and Strauss. For an extended critique of Meier's complex political rapprochement of Strauss and Schmitt, see Robert Howse, "The Use and Abuse of Leo Strauss in the Schmitt Revival on the German Right: The Case of Heinrich Meier" (forthcoming), a draft of which is available online at http://faculty.law.umich.edu/rhowse/Drafts_and_Publications/Meierbookrev.pdf.

22. Carl Schmitt, *Das Begriff des Politischen* (Berlin: Duncker und Humblot, [1932] 2002), 28. *The Concept of the Political* (Chicago: University Chicago Press, 1996), 28.

23. Schmitt, *Das Begriff des Politischen*, 29 (English, 28). Translations are mine as Schmitt quotes in Latin and Greek. Schmitt will on the next page of this text read "Love thine enemy as thyself" as referring to *inimicus*.

arguments. The first comes in his discussion of Hans Kelsen. At the time that Schmitt wrote the present volume, Kelsen was a leader in European jurisprudence, a prominent Austrian jurist and legal scholar as well as a highly influential member of the Austrian Constitutional Court. A student of Rudolf Stammler, Kelsen was a neo-Kantian by training and temperament, and shortly before the publication of *PT* had published *Das Problem der Souveränität und die Theorie des Völkerrechts*,[24] in which he set out the foundations for what he would later call a "pure theory of law," a theory of law from which all subjective elements would be eliminated.[25] Kelsen sought, in other words, a theory of law that would be universally valid for all times and all situations.[26]

Against this, Schmitt insists that "all law is situational law" (*PT*, 13). What he means by this is that in actual lived human fact it will always be the case that precisely at unpredictable times "the power of real life breaks through the crust of a mechanism that has become torpid by repetition" (*PT*, 15). Schmitt, in other words, requires that his understanding of law and politics respond to what he takes to be the fact of the ultimately unruly and unruled quality of human life. And if life can never be reduced or adequately understood by a set of rules, no matter how complex, then in the end, rule is of men and not of law—or rather that the rule of men must always existentially underlie the rule of law. For Schmitt, to pretend that one can have an ultimate "rule of law" is

24. Hans Kelsen, *Das Problem der Souveränität und die Theorie des Völkerrechts* [The Problem of Sovereignty and the Theory of International Law] (Tübingen: Mohr, 1920). See the articles on Kelsen in *European Journal of International Law* 9.2 (1998), especially that by Danilo Zolo.
25. A volume of articles comparing Schmitt and Kelsen has been published: *Hans Kelsen and Carl Schmitt: A Juxtaposition*, ed. Dan Diner and Michael Stolleis (Tel Aviv: Schriftenreihen des Instituts für deutsche Geschichte, University of Tel Aviv, 1999).
26. After 1933 Schmitt was apparently instrumental in the removal of Kelsen from the Law Faculty of the University of Köln. See D. Dyzenhaus, *Legality and Legitimacy: Carl Schmitt, Hans Kelsen, and Hermann Heller* (Oxford: Clarendon, 1997), 84.

to set oneself up to be overtaken by events at some unpredictable but necessarily occurring time and it is to lose the human element in and of our world.[27]

This is a powerful and important theme in Schmitt. It is not a claim that law is not centrally important to human affairs, but rather that in the end human affairs rest upon humans and cannot ever be independent of them. In his discussion of Locke, for instance, he criticizes Locke for saying that while the "law gives authority," he (Locke) "did not recognize that the law does not designate to whom it gives authority. It cannot be just anybody. . . ." (*PT*, 32).[28] Schmitt contrasts this to Hobbes's discussion (and in doing so brings out qualities often overlooked in discussions of Hobbes). He cites *Leviathan*, chapter 26, to the effect

27. One might in fact see much of the philosophical debates in the 1920s and 1930s as between those who sought to develop understandings that were independent of time and place and those who argued that all understanding needed to be grounded in concrete historical actuality. One might see Max Weber as the progenitor of both approaches. See the exceptional book by Michael Friedmann, *A Parting of the Ways: Carnap, Cassirer, and Heidegger* (Chicago: Open Court, 2000).

28. One might have thought here that Schmitt would have referred to Locke's discussion of the prerogative. Thus in the *Second Treatise on Government*, Locke writes: "What then could be done in this case to prevent the community from being exposed some time or other to eminent hazard, on one side or the other, by fixed intervals and periods, set to the meeting and acting of the legislative; but to entrust it to the prudence of some, who being present, and acquainted with the state of public affairs, might make use of this prerogative for the public good?" and later: "This power to act according to discretion, for the public good, without the prescription of the law, and sometimes even against it, is that which is called prerogative." Paragraphs 160–68 form a section entitled "Of Prerogative." There is a lot of secondary literature on this. See e.g. Clement Fatovic, "Constitutionalism And Contingency: Locke's Theory Of Prerogative," in *History of Political Thought* 25, no. 2 (2004), 276–97, as well as the discussion of prerogative in J. Dunn, *The political thought of John Locke: An Historical Account of the Argument of the 'Two Treatises of Government,'* (London: Cambridge University Press, 1969). See the short discussion in McCormick, "Dilemmas of Dictatorship," 237–38.

that sovereign power and not truth makes laws.[29] And he then drives the point home by citing Hobbes to the effect that "For Subjection, Command, Right and Power are accidents not of Powers but of Persons."[30] "Persons," for Hobbes, are beings constituted or authorized to play a certain role or part.[31]

Schmitt's insistence on the necessarily and irreducibly *human* quality of political and legal actions is key. Those who would elaborate a set of rules by which decisions can be made take human life out of politics: Schmitt is concerned to keep them. One might therefore see Schmitt as having raised in advance objections to central texts of contemporary liberalism, in particular the work of John Rawls in *A Theory of Justice* and especially in *Political Liberalism*, which invoke what Schmitt would have seen as an overly legalistic reliance on the courts.[32] Human society can thus never be made to rest on the determination and application of rules to individual situations. Decisions and judgments would always be necessary. In this Schmitt can be thought to be an initiator (albeit not recognized or known as such) of contemporary developments such as Critical Legal Studies on the Left and the Law and Economics movement on the Right.

Thus, for Schmitt the state is not cofounded with the legal order, and in exceptional situations the juristic order that prevails is

---

29. Schmitt quotes the Latin *Leviathan*, probably because the formulation is more succinct: *auctoritas, non veritas fecit legem.* The corresponding passage in English is: "though it be evident, truth is not therefore presently law; but because in all commonwealths in the world, it is part of the civil law: For though it be naturally reasonable; yet it is by the sovereign power that it is law . . ."

30. *Leviathan,* chapter 42. The context is the relation of civil to ecclesiastical authority.

31. See my "Seeing the Sovereign: Theatricality and Representation in Hobbes," in *Festschrift for Fred Dallmayr,* ed. Stephen Schneck (forthcoming).

32. See the critique by Sheldon S. Wolin, "Review of Rawls, Political Liberalism" in *Political Theory* 24.1 (February, 1996).

"not of the ordinary kind"[33] (*PT*, 12). The point therefore of this notion of sovereignty ultimately unconstrained by formal rules is to "create a juridical order" (*Recht zu schaffen*) under conditions that threaten anarchy.[34] The sovereign must decide both that a situation is exceptional and what to do about the exception in order to be able to create or recover a judicial order when the existing one is threatened by chaos.

The necessarily extraordinary quality of sovereignty is made clear in the analogy he uses to explain his point. He writes: "The exception in jurisprudence is analogous to the miracle in theology" (*PT*, 36). What does it mean to refer the "exception" to a "miracle"? Clearly, this appertains to "political theology." To move towards an answer one should look first at the author who remained Schmitt's touchstone. In chapter 37 of *Leviathan*, Hobbes first identifies a miracle as an occurrence when "the thing is strange, and the natural cause difficult to imagine" and then goes on to define it as "a work of God (besides His operation by the way of nature, ordained in the creation) done for the making manifest to His elect, the mission of an extraordinary minister for their salvation." [35] Hobbes' definition is apposite to Schmitt, as for him the "exception" is the *occasion for and of the revelation of the true nature of sovereignty*. Thus the sovereign does not for Schmitt only define the "exception"—he is also revealed by and in it, which is why Schmitt must refer to a "genuine" decision.

What would be wrong with at least trying to rest human affairs on the rule of law? Schmitt finds two major problems. The first comes from the epistemological relationship between the exception and the norm. Sovereignty is what Schmitt calls a *Grenzbegriff*,

---

33. Indeed, in such circumstances "the decision emanates from nothingness" (*PT*, 31–32). See the discussion in R. Howse, "From Legitimacy to Dictatorship—and Back Again," in Dyzenhaus *Law as Politics*, 60–65.

34. *PT*, 13. I have modified Schwab's translation, which is "to produce law."

35. Hobbes, *Leviathan*, chapter 37.

a "limiting" or "border" concept.[36] It thus looks in two directions, marking the line between that which is subject to law—where sovereignty reigns—and that which is not—potentially the space of the exception.[2] To look only to the rule of law would be to misunderstand the nature and place of sovereignty. For Schmitt, we only understand the nature of the juridical order by understanding sovereignty, that is, understanding that which opens on to the province of the exception.[38] This is because, he asserts, "the exception is more interesting than the rule" (*PT*, 15). As the Kierkegaard citation that Schmitt uses to support this claim argues, this is not because one cannot think about the rule or the "general," but because one does not notice anything in the general worth thinking about and thus our thought in this realm would be "without passion." (PT idem).

It is important to realize that one can only have an exception if one has a rule. Therefore the designation of something as an exception is in fact an assertion of the nature and quality of the rule. If, as director of the program I say "I am going to make an exception in your case and let you go on the exchange program to France despite the fact that you did not have the required grade point average," I am affirming both the rule and the fact that the rule is a human creation and hence does not control us automatically. I am also making a judgment that in this case, at this time, the good of all concerned indicates the need for this exception (and thus that I am not taking a bribe).

What though am I affirming in affirming the human quality of the rule? The claim about the exception and thus the grounding

---

36. Thus the exception is both part of and not part of the juridical order. See the useful discussion in Agamben, *State of Exception*, 24–26.

37. Schmitt, *Politisches Theologie*, 13.

38. See the striking and informative discussion in William Scheuerman, *Between the Norm and the Exception: The Frankfurt School and the Rule of Law* (Cambridge, Mass.: MIT Press, 1994), 330.

of rules on human actions is part of what Schmitt sees as the need
to defend the political. When Max Weber described the workings
of bureaucracy he asserted that in no case are bureaucratic (rationalized, rational-legal) relations, relations between human persons, between human beings. Bureaucracy is the form of social
organization that rests on norms and rules and not on persons. It
is thus a form of rule in which there is "'objective' discharge of
business . . . ; according to calculable rules and 'without regard
for persons.'"[39] What he meant is that it was in the nature of
modern civilization to remove the non-rational from societal
processes, replacing it by the formalism of abstract procedures.
(He did not think everything was always already like this—merely
that this was the tendency.) The disenchantment of the world
is for Weber the disappearance of politics, hence the disappearance of the human, hence the lessening of the role that the non-
rational and non-rule-governed play in the affairs of society. "Bureaucracy," he will proclaim, "has nothing to do with politics."

This is Schmitt's theme also. "Today nothing is more modern
than the onslaught against the political. . . . There must no longer
be political problems, only organizational-technical and economic-sociological ones" (*PT*, 65). In 1929, Schmitt will lecture
on Barcelona on this topic as "The Age of Neutralization and
Depoliticization."[40] The decline or disappearance of the political
is always for Schmitt a "political matter," as he makes clear in the
preface to the second edition of *PT*. If, however, the political is in
danger of disappearing as a human form of life, this can only be
because sovereignty as Schmitt understands it is increasingly not
a constituent part of our present world. Thus in his 1938 book on
Hobbes, he will write "the mechanization of the conception of

39. Max Weber, *Economy and Society* (Berkeley and Los Angeles: University of California
Press, 1967), 975.

40. I have had access to the text in its French translation, which is included in Carl Schmitt,
La notion du politique (Paris: Flammarion, 1992), 131–51.

the State has ended by bringing about the mechanization of the anthropological understanding of human beings."[41]

It is the growing realization of the importance of depoliticization, what Max Weber had called the "demagification [*Entzauberung*] of the world," that leads Schmitt in 1934 to note that his 1922 categories of juridical thinking had been too few. In the preface to the second edition, he writes: "I now distinguish between not two but three types of legal thinking; in addition to the normativist and the decisionist there is the institutional one"(*PT*, 2). He goes on to explain that whereas normativism thinks in terms of impersonal rules and decisionism thinks in terms of personal decisions, institutional thinking thinks in terms of organizations that transcend the personal sphere. Thus the state corresponds to normativism, political movements (*Bewegungen*) to decisionism, and the people (*Volk*) to institutionalism.[42] Institutionalism alone "leads to [a] pluralism . . . devoid of sovereignty" (*PT*, 3). In fact, public law under Wilhelminian and Weimar Germany was both a "deteriorated . . . normativism" *and* a "degenerate decisionism . . . [a] formless mixture, unsuitable for any structure. . . ." (*PT*, 3).

Schmitt, with explicit reference to Max Weber, sees danger in the increasing sense of the State as "a huge industrial plant" (*PT*, 65). Increasingly this plant "runs by itself . . . [and] the decisionistic and personalistic element in the concept of sovereignty is lost" (*PT*, 48). For Schmitt, this is a developmental process. As he lays it out in the Barcelona lecture, the history of the last 500 years in the

---

41. Schmitt, *Le Léviathan*, 100.

42. In the fall of 1933 Schmitt publishes *Staat, Bewegung, Volk: Die Dreigliedrung des politischen Einheit* [State, Movement, People: The Three Parts (*Glied* also means "limb") of Political Unity] (Hamburg: Hanseatische Verlagsanstalt, 1933). This book had an over-articulated sense of political society for some members of the Nazi Party and seems to have gotten him into trouble and led to the articles attacking him in the Gestapo organ *Das schwarze Korps* in 1936.

xxiv   Tracy B. Strong

West shows a common structure, even though as the controlling
force has changed, so also has what constitutes evidence, as well as
social elite. Thus in the sixteenth century the world was structured around an explicitly *theological* understanding with God and
the Scriptures as foundational certainties; this was replaced in the
next century by metaphysics and rational ("scientific") research
and in the eighteenth by ethical humanism, with its central notions of duty and virtue. In the nineteenth century economics
comes to dominate (although Schmitt is seen as a man of the
Right, he always took Marx completely seriously), and, finally, in
the twentieth century technology is the order of the day. And this
is at the core of his claim that ours is an age of "neutralisation and
depoliticization": whereas all previous eras had leaders and decision makers, the era of technology and technological progress has
no need of individual persons.[43] It is to call attention to this pro-
gression that Schmitt starts chapter three of *PT* with the second-
most-famous sentence of the book: "The central concepts of
modern state theory are all secularized theological concepts"[44]
(*PT*, 36; trans. modified).

What does this mean? Key here is Schmitt's understanding of
"secularized." Schmitt, who had been a student of Max Weber,
accepts the idea of the "demagification" or "disenchantment" of
the world. To say that all concepts in modern state theory are sec-

43. This periodization can be found explicitly in the Barcelona address and is implicit in the
first several pages of chapter three of *PT*; it is made explicit in shorter form in the 1934 preface to *PT*, 1–2. The stages are well discussed in Henning Ottmann, "Das Zeitalter der Neu-
tralisierungen und EntTotalisierungen: Carl Schmitts Theorie der Neuzeit," in *Carl Schmitt.
Der Begriff des Politischen. Ein Kooperativer Kommentar*, ed. Reinhard Mehring (Berlin: Akademie
Verlag, 2003), 156–69.
44. Schmitt, *Politisches Theologie*, 43. "Alle prägnanten Begriffe der modernen Staatslehre sind
säkularisierte theologische Begriffe." Translator George Schwab was faced with the difficult
task of rendering *prägnanten*; it means "concise, succinct," which is only partly caught by
Schwab's "significant." I have gone (with thanks for a consultation to William Arctander
O'Brien) for what I believe to be the meaning, rather than for a literal equivalent.

ularized theological concepts is not to want to restore to those concepts a theological dimension, but it is to point to the fact that what has been lost since the sixteenth ("theological") century has amounted to a hollowing-out of political concepts. They thus no longer have, as it were, the force and strength that they had earlier, and they are unable to resist the dynamics of technology. The consequence of Schmitt's notion of secularization is to try to restore to the concepts of sovereignty and political authority in a secular age the qualities that they had earlier.

Thus one might say that Schmitt is not a counter-revolutionary in a reactionary sort of way. He accepts that legitimacy in this age must be democratic—it certainly cannot be monarchical. And so although it is clear that he thinks that Maistre, Bonald, and Cortes got the problem right, their solutions (monarchy for the Frenchmen and dictatorship for the Spaniard) are unacceptable. As he notes on the last page of *PT*: "Those counterrevolutionary philosophers of the state . . . heightened the moment of the decision to such an extent that the notion of legitimacy, their starting point, was dissolved (*aufgehebt*). . . . This decisionism is essentially dictatorship, not legitimacy" (*PT*, 65–66).

While Schmitt has sympathies for these theorists over and against the bourgeois liberal thinkers that Cortes had stigmatized as a *clasa discutidora* (*PT*, 62),[45] the point of the analysis of the centrality of the exception for sovereignty is precisely to restore, in a democratic age, the element of transcendence that had been there in the sixteenth and even the seventeenth centuries— Hobbes, Schmitt believes, understood the problem exactly. Failing that, the triumph of non-political, inhuman technologizing will be inevitable. There is thus in Schmitt a challenge to those

---

45. Such, as Schmitt notes in *The Crisis of Liberal Democracy* (Cambridge, Mass.: MIT Press, 1985), 62, when presented with the choice "Christ or Barabbas [respond] with the proposal to adjourn or appoint a committee of investigation."

who would argue that politics in a democratic age can rest on discussion.[46] Such a claim is for him the privilege, as we saw, of the bourgeois "discussing classes."

There have been other theorists of secularization. Schmitt always associates himself with Weber on this matter, but it is the burden of a 1969 follow-up volume to *PT*, *Political Theology II*, to analyze and counter other such theorists. Of those he considers in that work, let us retain briefly his critique of Hans Blumenberg, whose 1966 *Die Legitimität der Neuzeit* [The legitimacy of the modern age][47] advanced a powerful theory of an independent modernity, apparently in critique of thinkers like Weber and Schmitt. Blumenberg wishes to defend reason in the contemporary age without having recourse to transcendental or teleological support. To vastly oversimplify a sweeping book, Blumenberg distinguishes three stages in Western history, each characterized by its own absolute: These have been "reality" where "nature" was the reference; "transcendence" where "God" was; and now "science," with "space and time." Thus for Blumenberg theories of secularization are misleading as they do not take into account the self-standing quality of each epoch.

While professing to admire the scope and ambition of the book, against it Schmitt notes that Blumenberg sees science as a *negation* of theology or transcendence. For him, this mixes together too many elements. Schmitt points out that he is not primarily concerned with metaphysical questions (he looks to the sixteenth rather than the seventeenth century), but simply the relation between the two most "highly evolved and structured organisms of 'Western rationalism,'" viz., the European State

---

46. See the discussion in Chantal Mouffe, "Carl Schmitt and the Paradoxes of Liberal Democracy," in Dyzenhaus, *Law as Politics*, 165–68.

47. Published by Suhrkamp, Frankfurt, 1966. An English translation has followed: *Hans Blumenberg, The Legitimacy of the Modern Age*, trans. Robert M. Wallace (Cambridge, Mass.: MIT Press, 1983).

based on the notion of a *ius publicum* and the Catholic Church with its juridical rationality. Consequent to this overly full pot Blumenberg tends to assimilate "right" to "law" and thus "legitimacy" to "legality," which in turn allows him to argue that the human desire to know (hence science) needs "no justification." Thus the immanence of value advocated by Blumenberg becomes for Schmitt simply a form of self-asserting "autism."[48]

For Schmitt, the secularization of theological concepts in the realm of sovereignty is rather to be understood as corresponding to the greatest progress in human rationality, progress that has occurred in and because of the State. This is "the distinction between enemy and criminal and from that the only possible foundation for a theory of State neutrality at the time of wars between other states."[49] Secularization, in other words, has made it possible for conflict to occur between enemies, but not between the legal and the criminal.[50]

But what is consequent to this understanding of secularization?[51] Three elements are involved. First is Schmitt's understanding of power. Political power is to be understood on the model of God's creation—which is how Hobbes had understood it. Power is to make something from that which is not something and thus is not subject to laid-down laws. This understanding of power clearly draws upon medieval theology, but it is the point of Schmitt's last chapter in *PT* to show that it is basically a modern understanding, most clearly formulated at the beginning of the nineteenth century by the French counter-revolutionary thinkers Joseph de Maistre, Louis de Bonald, and the Spanish theorist of

---

48. Schmitt, *Politisches Theologie II*, 84–89.

49. Schmitt, *Politisches Theologie II*, 86.

50. Schmitt will, towards the end of his life, write on *The Theory of the Partisan* in an insightful analysis of the transformations in warfare in the post-colonial period.

51. I am conscious in the next several paragraphs of the general influence of Etienne Balibar's introduction to Carl Schmitt, *Le Leviathan dans la doctrine de l'état de Thomas Hobbes*.

dictatorship and authority, Juan Donoso Cortes. These theorists wrote with the conscious intent to create the philosophical basis for opposition to the Enlightenment, which had, in their eyes, led to the chaos of the French Revolution and the disorders of modernity.

This points to the second element in Schmitt's conception of secularisation. The French revolution is the historically concrete manifestation of revolutionary myth, the myth of the creative power of the democratically equal populace. This is the basis of Schmitt's criticism of Rousseau, that the "general will" is substituted for the human will of a sovereign (*PT*, 46). To these understandings, it was necessary to oppose a myth of a hierarchically ordered and unified people, which the exceptional acts of the sovereign would instantiate. One might think of this as a kind of right-wing Leninism, where the Party is replaced by the *Volk* and the sovereign becomes the Party-in-action. The sovereign is the action of "us" against "them"—friends versus enemies.[52] This confrontation, however, must take place at the metaphysical level—that of one faith against another. For this reason the confrontation is one of "political theology."[53]

The last point indicates another element in Schmitt's conception of secularization. Schmitt is, in political matters, a realist, which is one of the reasons that people like Hans Morgenthau, the German-American theorist of the primacy of national interest in international relations, found him important. Schmitt here continues the line of thought initiated by Carl von Savigny. Savi-

---

52. All this, one should note, is quite consonant with a reading of Hobbes. See my "How to Write Scripture: Words and Authority in Thomas Hobbes," in *Critical Inquiry* (Autumn 1993) and Carl Schmitt, *Der Leviathan in der Staatslehre des Thomas Hobbes. Sinn und Feldschlag eines Symbols* (Stuttgart: Cotta'sche Buchhandlung, 1993) (1938), available to me in its French translation; see footnote 5.

53. See the discussion in Meier, *Carl Schmitt, Leo Strauss, and "The Concept of the Political"* (Chicago: University of Chicago Press, 2003), 77.

gny, an important legal theorist in the first half of the nineteenth century, argued that civil law acquired its character from the *Volksbewusstsein*—the common consciousness of the people—and was thus the product of the particular historically given qualities that a people might have. Hence, for him there was, in the Germany of that time, with its common language and customs, no real basis for different systems of law. For Savigny, the sovereign or legislator was the expresser of the *Volksbewusstsein*.[54] Schmitt, as we have seen, gives this part of Savigny's thought very strong emphasis.

Taken together, these elements in Schmitt's thought cast light on what we can surmise was the attraction of National Socialism. Schmitt came, as did Heidegger, from a rural, Catholic, petit-bourgeois upbringing. He describes his childhood, adolescence, and youth—the latter lasting for him until the end of World War I, during which he served as an officer and at the end of which he was thirty years old—as periods of getting rid of various influences. His Catholicism is "dis-placed" and "de-totalised"; greater Prussianness is "de-Hegelised." Likewise, during his "manhood," Weimar Germany is "de-Prussified."[55] While Catholicism was always to remain important to Schmitt, it is important to see in this self-description the portrait of a person whose ties to his various traditions are negative and are not replaced by a liberal faith in

---

54. This may make the question of Schmitt's anti-Semitic writings more complex. One might speak of anti-Judaism, meaning by that that Schmitt saw in German Judaism the kind of pluralism that he found incompatible with the commonalty of the *Volk* that he saw as essential to the political. In practice, however, certainly in the Third Reich, one could not be opposed to Judaism without being opposed to Jews.

55. This is Schmitt's account in his contribution to *Complexio Oppositorum. Uber Carl Schmitt*, ed. H. Quaritsch (Berlin, 1988), 105. See the discussion in Mehring, *Carl Schmitt*, 12–15, to which I owe this reference. It is worth noting that the flexibility of the German language permits Schmitt to construct neologisms in each of these cases: *entortet, entotalisiert, enthegelianisiert*, and *entpreusst*.

the future or in progress.[56] One has to read therefore his attacks on liberalism in conjunction with the accumulation of "de-" verbs.[57]

What then was the source of his attraction to Hitler? It was pretty clearly not an admiration of the particular qualities that the man had: even if one discounts the occasion, the disdain he expresses during his interrogation at Nuremberg is palpable.[58] One might rather say that Hitler appeared to him as something like the entity God had sent to perform a miracle—as in the citation from Hobbes above—and the miracle was the recovery of a this-world transcendence to sovereignty and thus the human realm of the political. From this understanding, the person *Hitler* was of no importance, and Schmitt's relation to Hitler's *actions* could only be the relation one has to a miracle: acceptance or rejection.

This is all the more likely as very rapidly Hitler seemed to many to behave like a true statesman in times of exception, legally in power and capable of making the hard, extra-legal decisions that were necessary. When Hitler and Goering ordered on June 30– July 2, 1934, the execution of all of the leadership of the SA, within two days almost all the press was congratulating them on having saved the country from civil war. Hindenburg sent (or was led to send) a telegram of thanks to the new Chancellor. Schmitt published on August 1, 1934, a newspaper article entitled *Der Führer schützt das Recht* [The Führer protects the legal order], de-

56. Schmitt is of course not the only person to be in this situation, nor was Heidegger. For a representative sense of the times, one can still profitably read J. B. Bury, *The Idea of Progress: An Inquiry into its Origin and Growth* (London: Macmillan, 1920).

57. And thus while left-wing anti-liberals can "learn from" Carl Schmitt, it is not completely clear that it is Carl Schmitt that they are learning. See Paul Piccone and G. L. Ulmen, "Introduction to Carl Schmitt," *Telos* 72 (Summer 1987), 14. See the material cited in Strong, "New Dimensions," 5–7.

58. Carl Schmitt, *Ex Captivate Salus*, 41: "He (Hitler) was so uninteresting to me that I don't even want to talk about it."

fending Hitler's actions.[59] Thus it is the *reality of taking power* and manifesting sovereignty in the use of power that attracted Schmitt: *his understanding of law required that he support Hitler.* It was not a question of succumbing to the charisma of a prophet, true or false.

In my preface to Schmitt's *The Concept of the Political,* I raised the question of the reason for his adherence to National Socialism. I rejected there the idea that he was blinded by ambition (though he was ambitious)[60] or that he misunderstood what Nazism was about (as if what it was about in 1933 was only one thing and obvious).[61] I suggested instead that Schmitt thought that the enemies of the regime were in fact (necessarily) enemies of what it meant to be German. I still think this is true, but then the problem with Schmitt is that he allows the notion of enemy to too easily define the notion of friend. Friends are harder to find, and easier to keep.

59. The matter is a bit more complex. Schmitt was identified with some elements of the SA and there is some evidence that he was specifically exempted from the purge by Goering. In a somewhat self-pitying and self-aggrandizing poem he wrote for his sixtieth birthday, "Gesang des Sechzigjährigen," he notes that he has been "three times in the belly of the fish." The first is 1934; the second, the attacks on him in 1936 in the Gestapo organ *Das schwarze Korps* (a moment he identifies to his interrogator in Nuremberg as when he "foreswore the devil"); and the last his interrogation after the war when he appears to believe that he might be hung. See Schmitt, *Ex Capitivate Salus, Textes et commentaires,* 171.

60. Cf. contra Mehring, *Carl Schmitt,* 61.

61. This is not to deny that it becomes, or *should* become, obvious at some time; when and how that happens is extremely important. Additionally, the experience of not having been obvious affects the recognition of the obvious.

As an example of the kind of argument that I do not think can be sustained on the question of the reasons for Schmitt's adherence to Nazism, see Julien Freund, "Préface," in Carl Schmitt, *La notion du politique* (Paris: Flammarion, 1992), 10ff, where Freund refers ambiguously to the anti-semitism and makes Schmitt out to be a version of Max Weber. For Freund, the links speak in favor of Schmitt. Jürgen Habermas in *The Philosophical Discourse of Modernity: Twelve Lectures* (Cambridge, Mass.: MIT Press, 1987) makes the same link in condemnation of Schmitt. See Duncan Kelly, *The State of the Political Conceptions of Politics and the State in the Thought of Max Weber, Carl Schmitt, and Franz Neumann* (Oxford: Oxford University Press, 2003).

In the larger context of Schmitt's postwar writings there would be much more to be said about the relation of the political to the theological in Carl Schmitt. He notes, as had Hobbes, that there is in Christianity a dangerous tendency to introduce rebellion into the political realm. Hobbes and Hegel in particular try to tame this tendency and make use of it in the political realm, by linking religion to the State. Schmitt's approval is strong: they are what he calls *katechontes*, defined by St. Paul in 2 Thessalonians, 2: 6–7 as "those who hold" back the Apocalypse—thus for Schmitt those who slow down the complete neutralization of what is important about religion for the State.[62] The greatest *katechon* has been the Catholic Church and Schmitt thus finds himself in alliance with the Grand Inquisitor in Dostoevsky.[63]

What does it mean to find oneself on the side of the Grand Inquisitor? It is to claim that the Right has gotten the problem of modern politics correct, even if what it has sometimes proposed to do about it (as with Maistre, Bonald, and Cortes) has not always been on target or on the only target. But with this, what now? One can only note in this day and age, as William Scheuerman reminds us,[64] that the United States today has on its books a sufficient number of emergency powers, established sine die, to allow the executive free hand at the rule of all aspects of this country. The present US administration has ruled that certain prisoners in

---

62. The *katechon* reappears in the thought of Dietrich Bonhoeffer, but not as a being exempt from sin, as he tends to in Schmitt's work. See the discussion in Wolfgang Palaver, "Collective Security: Opportunities and Problems from the Perspective of Catholic Social Teaching" in *Peace in Europe—Peace in the World: Reconciliation, Creation and International Institutions*. Hrsg. von Iustitia et Pax—Österreichische Kommission (Iustitia et Pax Dokumentation 4) (Wien: Südwind-Verlag, 2003), 86–102.

63. I am helped in part by the work of Wolfgang Palaver, "Carl Schmitt, mythologue politique," 2002.

64. Scheuerman in *Boston Review*, 2001.

the "war against terrorism" have in effect no status at all, not even that of a person charged with a crime.[65]

Schmitt had followed a sovereign for a while and then renounced him. (In his testimony at Nuremberg he identifies 1936 as the date when he "renounced the devil," presumably after the attack on him in *Das schwarze Korps*.)[66] In *Benito Cereno*, the resolution was not so easy. The chilling and uncompromising end to Melville's account of these matters is as follows:

> As for the black—whose brain, not body, had schemed and led the revolt, with the plot—his slight frame, inadequate to that which it held, had at once yielded to the superior muscular strength of his captor, in the boat. Seeing all was over, he uttered no sound, and could not be forced to. His aspect seemed to say: since I cannot do deeds, I will not speak words. Put in irons in the hold, with the rest, he was carried to Lima. During the passage Don Benito did not visit him. Nor then, nor at any time after, would he look at him. Before the tribunal he refused. When pressed by the judges he fainted. On the testimony of the sailors alone rested the legal identity of Babo. And yet the Spaniard would, upon occasion, verbally refer to the Negro, as has been shown; but look on him he would not, or could not.
>
> Some months after, dragged to the gibbet at the tail of a mule, the black met his voiceless end. The body was burned to ashes; but for many days, the head, that hive of subtlety, fixed on a pole in the Plaza, met, unabashed, the gaze of the whites; and across the Plaza looked toward St. Bartholomew's church, in whose vaults slept then, as now, the recovered bones of Aranda; and across the Rimac bridge looked toward the monastery, on Mount Agonia without; where, three months after being dismissed by the court, Benito Cereno, borne on the bier, did, indeed, follow his leader.

Tracy B. Strong
University of California, San Diego
Lyon, France April 2005

---

65. Agamben, *State of Exception*, 4, compares their situation to those of Jews in Nazi contentration camps.

66. Schmitt, *Ex Captivate Salus*, 41.

Selected English Language Bibliography

Agamben, G. *State of Exception*. Chicago: University of Chicago Press, 2005.

Balakrishnan, G. *The Enemy: An Intellectual Portrait of Carl Schmitt*. London: Verso, 2000.

Bendersky, J. W. *Carl Schmitt: Theorist for the Reich*. Princeton: Princeton University Press, 1983.

Caldwell, P. C. *Popular Sovereignty and the Crisis of German Constitutional Law: The Theory and Practice of Weimar Constitution*. Durham, N.C.: Duke University Press, 1997.

Cardozo Law Review 21, nos. 5–6 (May 2000) [issue dedicated to Schmitt].

Cristi, R. *Carl Schmitt and Authoritarian Liberalism*. Cardiff: University of Wales Press, 1998.

Diner, D. and M. Stolleis, eds. *Hans Kelsen and Carl Schmitt: A Juxtaposition*. Tel Aviv: Schriftenreihen des Instituts für deutsche Geschichte, University of Tel Aviv, 1999.

Dyzenhaus, D. *Legality and Legitimacy: Carl Schmitt, Hans Kelsen, and Hermann Heller*. Oxford: Clarendon, 1997.

Dyzenhaus, D., ed. *Law as Politics: Carl Schmitt's Critique of Liberalism*. Durham, N.C.: Duke University Press, 1998.

Holmes, S. *The Anatomy of Antiliberalism*. Cambridge, Mass.: Harvard University Press, 1993.

Howse, R. "From Legitimacy to Dictatorship—and Back Again: Leo Strauss's Critique of the Anti-Liberalism of Carl Schmitt." In *Legality and Legitimacy: Carl Schmitt, Hans Kelsen, and Hermann Heller*, edited by D. Dyzenhaus, 56–91. Oxford: Clarendon, 1997.

Kennedy, E. "Carl Schmitt and the Frankfurt School." *Telos* 71 (Spring 1987), 37–66.

Lilla, M. "The Enemy of Liberalism." *New York Review of Books* 44, no. 8 (May 15, 1997).

Meier, H. *Carl Schmitt and Leo Strauss: The Hidden Dialogue*. Chicago: University of Chicago Press, 1995.

Meier, H. *Carl Schmitt, Leo Strauss, and "The Concept of the Political."* Chicago: University of Chicago Press, 2003.

Mouffe, Ch., ed. *The Challenge of Carl Schmitt*. London: Verso, 1999.

Müller, J. W. *A Dangerous Mind: Carl Schmitt in Post-War European Thought*. New Haven, Conn.: Yale University Press, 2002.

Piccone, P., and G. L. Ulmen, eds. *Telos* 72 (Summer 1987).

Preuss, Ulrich K. *Constitutional Revolution: The Link Between Constitutionalism and Progress*. Boston: Humanities, 1995.

Rasch, W. "Conflict as a vocation. Carl Schmitt and the possibilities of Politics." In *Theory, Culture & Society* 17 (2000): 1–32.

Scheuerman, W. *Between the Norm and the Exception: The Frankfurt School and the Rule of Law*. Cambridge, Mass.: MIT Press, 1994.

Scheuerman, W. *Carl Schmitt: The End of Law*. Lanham: Rowman & Littlefield, 1999.

Scheuerman, W. "Down on Law.: The complicated legacy of the authoritarian jurist Carl

Schmitt." *Boston Review* [review of Balakrishnan, *The Enemy: An Intellectual Portrait of Carl Schmitt*] (April–May 2001).

Schwab, G. *The Challenge of the Exception: An Introduction to the Political Ideas of Carl Schmitt between 1921 and 1936.* New York: Greenwood Press, 1989.

Strong, T. B. "New Dimensions in the Debate Over Carl Schmitt." Introduction to *The Concept of the Political*, Carl Schmitt. Chicago: Univesity of Chicago Press, 1995. See also the citations there.

Wolin, R. "Carl Schmitt, political existentialism and the total state." *Theory and Society* 19, no. 2 (1990): 2, 389–416.

Wolin, R. "Carl Schmitt, the Conservative Revolutionary: Habitus and the Aesthetics of Horror." *Political Theory* 20, no. 3 (August 1992): n424–47.

Introduction

George Schwab

Carl Schmitt is undoubtedly the most controversial German legal and political thinker of the twentieth century. If his friends and foes agree on nothing else, they both acknowledge his brilliance. Even his detractors concede that he is one of the outstanding intellects of our time. Why, then, is he so little known in the English-speaking world? Who is Carl Schmitt?

I

The father of numerous pivotal political ideas—including the "total" (or, as it was later known, "totalitarian") state, which figured in the thought of Franz Neumann, Herbert Marcuse, and Hannah Arendt, among others; the friend-enemy criterion of politics, a central notion in the writings of such political realists as Hans Morgenthau; and the thesis that democracy negates liberalism and liberalism negates democracy, an idea echoed by the New Left—Carl Schmitt was born in 1888 in a devout Catholic family in the predominantly Protestant town of Plettenberg in

Westphalia.[1] The young Schmitt greatly admired his church and was proud of its victory over Bismarck in the *Kulturkampf* controversy that had officially come to an end in 1887. Though his family expected him to prepare for the priesthood, he opted for law instead, beginning his university studies in Berlin in 1907 and receiving his doctorate in jurisprudence from the University of Strasbourg in 1910.

World War I was decisive for the formation of Schmitt's conception of the state. Before the war he was emotionally and intellectually governed by the Catholic church and espoused a neo-Kantian construction of the state compatible with his religious beliefs. He was convinced that the Church was a universal spiritual entity with no equal, and he regarded this as the appropriate source for the determination of right. Right for him thus preceded the state, and the purpose of the latter was to realize the former; the proper order of things was right, state, individual.[2]

The realities of World War I shattered the neo-Kantian abstraction that had governed Schmitt's *Weltanschauung*, and he began to veer toward a starker political realism. Whereas for Schmitt the neo-Kantian the state was governed by right, for Schmitt the realist it was governed by the ever-present possibility of conflict.[3] This conception of the state became the focal point of his thinking. In contrast to Hegel, for whom the state was the realization of the highest form of existence, Schmitt perceived

---

1. For detailed biographical information see Joseph W. Bendersky, *Carl Schmitt: Theorist for the Reich* (Princeton, 1983), pp. 3–20 *passim*, and George Schwab, *The Challenge of the Exception: An Introduction to the Political Ideas of Carl Schmitt between 1921 and 1936* (Berlin, 1970), pp. 13–28 *passim*.

2. Carl Schmitt, *Der Wert des Staates und die Bedeutung des Einzelnen* (Tübingen, 1914), pp. 2, 44–45.

3. See Joseph H. Kaiser, "Einige Umrisse des deutschen Staatsdenkens seit Weimar, Ulrich Scheuner zum Gedenken" (Sonderdruck), *Archiv des öffentlichen Rechts* 108/1 (1983): 8.

the role of the state as the securing of conditions under which citizens could pursue their private wills. It is not surprising, therefore, that he returned again and again in his writings to Thomas Hobbes's "mutual Relation between Protection and Obedience," and shared with Hobbes the belief that *autoritas, non veritas facit legem.* The one who has authority can demand obedience—and it is not always the legitimate sovereign who possesses this authority. It was this belief in the need to support the legally constituted authority that led Schmitt to participate in the Nazi adventure between 1933 and 1936.

This decision is critical for understanding why Schmitt is so little known in the English-speaking world. In his endeavor to develop for the Third Reich an authoritarian theory of the state that would be distinctly Schmittian (and thus would bear little resemblance to the totalitarian one-party state that was emerging in Germany), he made a number of truly shocking compromises with the regime. Had he not participated in the Nazi rule between 1933 and 1936, or at least not sunk to the depth to which he did on the Jewish question, for example,[4] his voluminous and gifted intellectual output of the Weimar period would certainly have been assessed differently.[5] As things now stand, many scholars continue to view his Weimar output from the perspective of

4. See George Schwab, "Carl Schmitt: Political Opportunist?," *Intellect* 103 (February 1975): 334–337.
5. See George Schwab, "Schmitt Scholarship," *Canadian Journal of Political and Social Theory* 4/2 (Spring–Summer 1980): 149–155; also Joseph W. Bendersky, "Carl Schmitt Confronts the English-speaking World," *Canadian Journal of Political and Social Theory* 2/3 (Fall 1978): 125–135.

the Third Reich, as undermining the republic and preparing the way for Hitler's Germany.[6]

Because Schmitt was regarded in England and America as simply a Nazi theoretician, there seemed to be no scholarly reason for translating his work. In fact, it was not until 1976 that the first translation of the work of this "Hobbes of the twentieth century"[7] appeared in English. This was *The Concept of the Political*, the work in which Schmitt advanced the friend-enemy criterion of politics, which he had originally developed in 1927.[8] Before the appearance of this translation, the only full-length study of Schmitt's ideas to appear in English was *The Challenge of the Exception: An Introduction to the Political Ideas of Carl Schmitt between 1921 and 1936*, which appeared in 1970.[9] This has since been complemented by the work of Joseph W. Bendersky, whose *Carl Schmitt: Theorist for the Reich* appeared in 1983.[10]

6. See, for example, recent reviews of Bendersky's study by Gordon A. Craig, "Decision, Not Discussion," *Times Literary Supplement*, August 12, 1983; and Martin Jay, "Carl Schmitt: Theorist for the Reich," *Journal of Modern History* 53/3 (September 1984): 558–561. Stephen Holmes, "Carl Schmitt: Theorist for the Reich," *American Political Science Review* 77/4 (December 1983): 1067, asserts that Schmitt is a "theorist who consciously embraced evil and whose writings cannot be studied without moral revulsion and intellectual distress." A contrary view is expressed in G. L. Ulmen's review in *Telos* 59 (Spring 1984): 210–212. See also Ellen Kennedy's review in *History of Political Thought* 4/3 (Winter 1983): 579–589.

7. The title of Helmut Rumpf's book is revealing: *Carl Schmitt und Thomas Hobbes: Ideelle Beziehungen und aktuelle Bedeutung mit einer Abhandlung über: die Frühschriften Carl Schmitts* (Berlin, 1972); see also Leo Strauss, "Comments on Carl Schmitt's *Der Begriff des Politischen*" (1932), reprinted in Carl Schmitt, *The Concept of the Political*, trans. George Schwab (New Brunswick, NJ, 1976), pp. 81–105.

8. Schmitt's *Concept of the Political* appeared first in the *Archiv für Sozialwissenschaft und Sozialpolitik* 58/1 (1927): 1–33. My translation was based on the expanded work, which appeared in 1932.

9. See note 1.

10. For comprehensive bibliographies of Schmitt's work, as well as most publications related to him and his ideas, see Piet Tommissen, "Carl-Schmitt-Bibliographie," in *Festschrift für Carl Schmitt zum 70. Geburtstag*, ed. Hans Barion et al. (Berlin, 1959), pp. 273–330; "Ergänzungsliste zur Carl-Schmitt-Bibliographie vom Jahre 1959," in *Epirrhosis: Festgabe für Carl Schmitt*, ed. Hans Barion et al., 2 vols. (Berlin, 1968), pp. 739–778; "Zweite Fortsetzungsliste der C.S.—Bibliographie vom Jahre 1959," *Cahiers Vilfredo Pareto* 16/44 (July 1978): 187–238.

There are a number of reasons for adding a translation of
Political Theology to the list of Schmitt's works in English.[11] First,
a translation of *Political Theology* will contribute to a deeper understanding of the political and constitutional history of the Weimar
period in general and of Schmitt's work in particular. Second,
Political Theology is a necessary complement to *The Concept of the
Political* in explaining Schmitt's understanding of state, sovereignty,
and politics. Third, the work has withstood the test of time; it
continues to be relevant to our understanding of the functioning
of the sovereign state.

II

This introduction will focus on Schmitt's definition of sovereignty
and on how he applied this concept in his efforts to save the
Weimar state. As already mentioned, World War I was decisive
in forming Schmitt's conception of the state and, hence, of sovereignty. Concerned about the conditions that obtained in the
wake of Germany's defeat and the centrifugal forces that pulled
at the new republic, Schmitt sought a theoretical construct with
which to analyze and combat these challenges. He adopted the
view that "all significant concepts of the modern theory of the
state are secularized theological concepts."[12] But he went on to

11. *Politische Theologie: Vier Kapitel zur Lehre von der Souveränität* first appeared in 1922
(Munich and Leipzig); a second edition, with a new foreword, appeared in 1934. The
present translation is based on the 1934 edition. A third printing based on the second
edition appeared in Berlin in 1979. The first three chapters of this work also appeared
under the title "Soziologie des Souveränitätsbegriffes und politische Theologie," in
Erinnerungsgabe für Max Weber, vol. 2, ed. Melchior Palyi (Munich and Leipzig, 1923),
pp. 3–35.
12. For recent discussions of this formulation and some of its implications, see Ernst-
Wolfgang Böckenförde, "Politische Theorie und politische Theologie," in *Der Fürst dieser
Welt: Carl Schmitt und die Folgen*, Religionstheorie und politische Theologie, vol. 1, ed.
Jacob Taubes (Munich and Zurich, 1983), pp. 16–25; and José Maria Beneyto, *Politische
Theologie als politische Theorie* (Berlin, 1983), especially pp. 62–89.

show that even though a concept such as the omnipotent lawgiver could be traced back to that of the omnipotent God, the meaning of the concept had changed profoundly over the centuries.

Whereas the omnipotent lawgiver was still associated with the personal element of rule in the seventeenth and eighteenth centuries, the personal factor had been dissipated by the nineteenth and twentieth centuries. In reaction to monarchical legitimacy, efforts were made to divide political power, to split it up, to set it against itself. This fragmentation occurred under the impact of such ideas as democratic legitimacy; the division of power; the notion that power must be checked by power, which is a central tenet of constitutional liberalism; and the idea that the sovereignty of law should replace the sovereignty of men. Although Schmitt was prepared to accept modern constitutional developments, he was determined to reinstate the personal element in sovereignty and make it indivisible once more.

To him this was essential, not because he harbored a romantic yearning for the past or because he valued contrariness for its own sake, but because he considered the restoration of the personal element vital for the preservation of the modern constitutional state. Convinced that the state is governed by the ever-present possibility of conflict, he held that resolute action was necessary to combat threats, for the state's raison d'être was to maintain its integrity in order to ensure order and stability.

Given the threat of conflict and the uncertainty and distress this could engender, Schmitt focused his attention on crises in a state's existence. A crisis, according to him, is "more interesting than the rule" because "it confirms not only the rule but also its existence, which derives only from the exception." He was quick to add, nevertheless, that because the exception is "distinguishable from a juristic chaos," it must be construed as a juristic problem and as such made subject to juristic considerations. It was on this critical issue that he differed from neo-Kantians such as Hans Kelsen who, in endeavoring to construct a legal system that was scientifically airtight, banished the exception. Because Schmitt viewed such endeavors as exercises in futility, he raised a number of questions in order to subject the exception to juristic consideration: Which authority in the state is competent to decide that an exception is at hand? Which is competent to determine the measures to be undertaken in case of an exception to safeguard the political unity? Finally, which authority in the state is competent to conclude that order and stability have been restored?

In answering these questions, Schmitt attempted to challenge those jurists who equated the state with the legal order—who considered the state to be a "system of ascriptions to a last point of ascription and to a last basic norm." How, he asked, can legal ideas be expected to realize themselves? How can an exception be subsumed in such a legal configuration when in reality the details of the exception "cannot be anticipated, nor can one spell out what may take place in such a case." In short, "the exception," said Schmitt, "is that which cannot be subsumed." On the basis of this conclusion Schmitt dismissed liberal constitutional endeavors to regulate the exception as precisely as possible.

In order to make the concept of sovereign power relevant to the modern state, Schmitt felt compelled to liberate the concept not only from the so-called scientific system of norms but also from obfuscations and repressions brought about by liberal constitutional thought and parlance. For Schmitt the sovereign authority not only was bound to the normally valid legal order but also transcended it. As I put it elsewhere, his sovereign slumbers in normal times but suddenly awakens when a normal situation threatens to become an exception.[13] The core of this authority is its exclusive possession of the right of, or its monopoly of, political decision making. Thus Schmitt's definition: "Sovereign is he who decides on the exception." In this critical moment sovereign power reveals itself in its purest form.[14] Subsumed under Schmitt's definition are, of course, the sovereign's ability to decide "what must be done to eliminate" the exception and the ability to decide whether order and stability have been restored and normality regained—attributes of sovereignty that were explicit in the works of such thinkers as Bodin, Hobbes, and Donoso Cortés, according to Schmitt. The restoration of order and stability was the precondition for the reinstatement of norms. According to Schmitt, "for a legal system to make sense, a normal situation must exist, and he is sovereign who definitely decides whether this normal situation actually exists."

Arguing that the essence of sovereign power precludes it from being subject to law all the time, even in exceptional times, Schmitt maintained that the endeavors of the sovereign can only be understood in the overall context of the legal order within which this authority operates. He accepted the new German order and desired to strengthen it against the centrifugal forces that had developed in the republic; he considered the emergency provision of the Weimar constitution adequate for meeting crises; and as a close examination of his writings of the Weimar period

13. Schwab, *The Challenge of the Exception*, p. 50.
14. See also Franz Neumann, "Approaches to the Study of Political Power" (1950), in *The Democratic and the Authoritarian State: Essays in Political and Legal Theory*, 2d printing (Glencoe, IL, 1964), p. 17. There is no question, in Neumann's view, that "the study of . . . emergency situations will yield valuable hints as to where political power actually resides in 'normal' periods."

will show, he acknowledged the interdependence of the state and the constitution. According to his view, interpreting the provisions of the constitution in a manner that strengthened the state's raison d'être, assuring citizens of order and stability, would enable the constitutional order of the state to function normally.

III

The emergency provision of the Weimar constitution was, of course, the famous article 48. Inasmuch as Schmitt's focus in *Political Theology* is on the *theory* of sovereignty, we must turn to his other writings for an appreciation of how he translated his theoretical construction into concrete terms. Mindful of how easily an emergency provision such as article 48 could be abused, Schmitt published a comprehensive study of dictatorship shortly before the appearance of *Political Theology*.[15] There he traced the history of dictatorship and concluded that it can be categorized into two forms: commissarial and sovereign. A sovereign dictatorship utilizes a crisis to abrogate the existing constitution in order to bring about a "condition whereby a constitution [that the sovereign dictator] considers to be a true constitution will become possible," whereas a commissarial dictatorship endeavors to restore order so that the existing constitution can be revived and allowed to function normally.[16] Schmitt showed that article 48 accorded with the commissarial type of dictatorship, stressing the continuation of the Weimar constitutional order, critical interruptions not-

15. *Die Diktatur: Von den Anfängen des modernen Souveränitätsgedankens bis zum proletarischen Klassenkampf* (Munich and Leipzig, 1921). A second edition appeared in 1928; the third and fourth editions, published in Berlin in 1964 and 1978, respectively, are primarily reprints of the expanded, second edition.
16. Ibid., pp. 136–137.

withstanding. These critical interruptions were what concerned Schmitt; his explication of article 48, which provoked much controversy, centered on two sentences of the second section of the article:

If, in the German Reich, public security and order are considerably disturbed or endangered, the Reichspräsident may undertake necessary measures to restore public security and order, and if necessary may intervene with the aid of armed forces. For this purpose he may suspend, temporarily, in part or entirely, the basic rights as provided in articles 114, 115, 117, 118, 123, 124, and 153.

Arguing that because it is impossible to anticipate the form of an exception, and hence impossible to prescribe the president's precise course of action, Schmitt maintained that it could not have been the intention of the founding fathers of the republic to restrict or hamper presidential action taken to restore order. He thus raised the question of whether the second sentence modified the first, as leading exponents of the legalistic view insisted: *enumeratio, ergo limitatio.*

By tracing the origins of article 48 to the Constituent Assembly, Schmitt established that the two sentences had been drawn up separately by different committees and that the difficulty in interpreting the second section stemmed from the modification of the first sentence, which reflected the reluctance of committee members to mention "armed force" at the beginning of the article. Hence the original version of the core of the first sentence—"the Reichspräsident may intervene . . . with the aid of armed forces and undertake necessary measures to restore public security and order"—was changed to read "the Reichspräsident may undertake necessary measures to restore public security and order, and if necessary may intervene with the aid of armed forces." The second sentence, beginning with "For this purpose," remained unchanged, and in its original (and, in Schmitt's view, proper) context should have read: "For the purpose of reestablishing public security and order the Reichspräsident may undertake measures and may suspend certain basic rights." Following this line of reasoning, Schmitt argued that the second sentence says nothing about what can be done aside from suspending basic rights. The most it says is that if measures of the Reichspräsident include suspending basic rights, then the suspension is limited to certain enumerated rights.[17] Schmitt's loose or latitudinarian interpretation was resolutely opposed by the overwhelming majority, by those who adhered to the strict or legalistic interpretation of article 48, which held that the articles the president could suspend were *only* the enumerated ones.

Committed to preserving and strengthening the Weimar state and mindful of the threat from the Nazis and the Communist party, Schmitt further antagonized the majority by injecting into legal considerations his friend-enemy distinction. Advanced originally in 1927, this criterion of politics was commonly thought to be applicable to relations between or among states.[18] But according to Schmitt, it was relevant to domestic affairs as well:

The endeavor of a normal state consists above all in assuring total peace within the state. . . . To create tranquility, security, and order and thereby establish the normal situation is the prerequisite for legal norms to be valid. Every norm presupposes a normal situation, and no norm can be valid in an entirely abnormal situation. As long as a state is a political entity, this requirement for internal peace compels it in critical situations to decide also upon the domestic enemy.[19]

17. Ibid. (2d ed.), pp. 224–226. See also Schwab, *The Challenge of the Exception*, pp. 37–43.
18. Schmitt, *The Concept of the Political*.
19. Ibid., p. 46.

In the context of the Weimar constitutional order, anticon-
stitutional parties could paralyze the government by a vote of
no confidence in the Reichstag (article 54). In possession of an
ordinary majority in the Reichstag, such parties could enact any
ordinary law (article 68), and a qualified majority—in the view
of leading interpreters of the constitution, including Gerhard
Anschütz and Richard Thoma—could even bring about fundamental constitutional revisions (article 76).[20] Finally, there was
nothing to prevent an unconstitutional party that had come to
power from legally closing the door behind itself and denying
other parties the right to compete and gain power.

Schmitt rejected the prevailing view that it was not in the spirit
of liberalism to deny any party the right to compete for power.
He feared that existing electoral methods could and would be
exploited by revolutionaries of the left and right in their quest
for power; such a concrete challenge demanded a realistic response. Building on his criterion of sovereignty as the ability to
decide on the exception, including the decision to designate the
domestic enemy, and on his latitudinarian interpretation of article
48, Schmitt formulated in the critical year 1932 his notion of the
"equal chance," which aimed at banishing extreme political
movements from the political arena.

Arguing in *Legalität und Legitimität* that every constitution em-
bodies principles that are sacrosanct, principles that may include
liberalism, private property, and religious toleration, Schmitt opposed the view of those who interpreted the constitution in a

---

20. See Anschütz, *Die Verfassung des Deutschen Reichs vom 11 August 1919*, 11th ed. (Berlin,
1929), pp. 351–352, and *Kommentar zur Reichsverfassung*, 14th ed. (1932), pp. 404ff. See
also, Thoma, "Die Funktionen der Staatsgewalt," in *Handbuch des Deutschen Staatsrechts*,
vol. 2, ed. Gerhard Anschütz and Richard Thoma (Tübingen, 1932), p. 154.

"value-free" and "legalistic" fashion.[21] He acknowledged that such an interpretation might be appropriate in countries where political parties accept the legitimacy of the constitution and hence adhere to what are commonly known as the rules of the game, as in England, for example. There, as Lord Balfour noted in his introduction to Walter Bagehot's *The English Constitution,* "[the] whole political machinery presupposes a people so fundamentally at one that they can safely afford to bicker; and so sure of their own moderation that they are not dangerously disturbed by the never-ending din of political conflict." Because such conditions did not exist in Germany, Schmitt argued, a value-neutral and legalistic interpretation of the constitution facilitated its subversion. Having once gained power, a militant party would not hesitate to exercise sovereignty in order to transform itself into the state.[22] By insisting that a constitution by definition does not aim at its self-destruction, Schmitt concluded that an equal chance should be accorded only to those parties committed to the preservation of the existing constitutional order. In the crisis year of 1932, therefore, he saw no alternative to the full assertion by President Hindenburg of his constitutional prerogatives and sovereign powers to save the state.[23]

IV

Because he shared with his mentor Thomas Hobbes the belief that man is basically dangerous and that his primary goal is

21. *Legalität und Legitimität* (Munich and Leipzig, 1932; Berlin, 1969, 1980).
22. Ibid., pp. 33, 35, 41–42, 48–50.
23. See my introduction to Schmitt, *The Concept of the Political*, pp. 13–16; also Joseph W. Bendersky, "Carl Schmitt in the Summer of 1932: A Reexamination," *Cahiers Vilfredo Pareto* 16/44 (July 1978): 51–52; and Paul Hirst, "Socialism, Pluralism, and Law," *International Journal of the Sociology of Law* 2 (1985): 180–181 *passim.*

George Schwab

physical security, Schmitt opted for a strong state that would ensure order, peace, and stability. Abstracted from his numerous writings, especially those of the Weimar period, Schmitt's political theory can be summarized in the following propositions: By virtue of its possession of a monopoly on politics, the state is the only entity able to distinguish friend from enemy and thereby demand of its citizens the readiness to die. This claim on the physical life of its constituents distinguishes the state from, and elevates it above, all other organizations and associations. To maintain order, peace, and stability, the legally constituted sovereign authority is supported by an armed force and a bureaucracy operating according to rules established by legally constituted authorities.[24]

With the Weimar order in mind, Schmitt suggested in his writings that the condition of his acceptance of political parties and parliament would be that they be united with the sovereign—the popularly elected president—in seeking the solutions necessary for the welfare of the entire civil society. In his endeavor to defuse political tensions in society, he rejected the idea of permitting negative political parties to utilize bourgeois electoral methods to capture the state and also opted for a separation of church and state. Arguing that the church habitually meddled in affairs beyond its concern and that theology opened many avenues for politicizing society, Schmitt finally echoed the exhortation of Albericus Gentilis: *Silete, theologi, in munere alieno!*[25]

Once Weimar had regained a measure of stability, attention could be focused on devising a constitutional order that would once and for all drain civil society of political forces that could

24. Carl Schmitt, "Starker Staat und gesunde Wirtschaft" (1932), *Volk und Reich* 2 (1933): 93.
25. Carl Schmitt, *Der Nomos der Erde im Völkerrecht des Jus Publicum Europaeum*, 2d printing (Berlin, 1974), pp. 96, 131.

challenge the state's monopoly on politics. Schmitt hoped to achieve this by devising a constitutional order based on institutions or concrete orders, in particular the variety associated with Maurice Hauriou.

The mere fact that Schmitt toyed with such an idea toward the end of the Weimar period, and that he elaborated it in 1934, is proof that he realized the limits of decisionism. However appropriate he considered decisionism in exceptional times, Schmitt's obsession with stability and physical security led him to conclude that a sound constitutional order must be based on fundamentally tranquil social pillars. He argued that legally recognized institutions such as religious associations and the professional civil service, or interest groups organized along professional or occupational lines, would ensure the continuity of the societal order more easily than a political system, which could be easily destroyed. This constitutional order as originally conceived would have been based on the principle of the legitimacy of the Weimar president and (anticipating some of the present-day "legitimation through procedure" discussions) on the principle of legitimacy of concrete orders. Every institution had its own legal existence established by the institutionalization of practices in light of a concept of justice based on the interaction of members in a given order. The more solidly an order is entrenched, the less likely it is that the sovereign authority will venture to intervene in normal times.

The legitimacy of concrete orders notwithstanding, Schmitt's construction was not meant to fragment the state. As the "institution of institutions," the state in this configuration embraces and protects the societal institutions. To discuss and resolve problems of mutual interest and arrive at definite decisions, the organized interests would meet with the sovereign authority in a parliament.[26] Just as the sovereign would, under ordinary circumstances, have no reason to violate the orders, it would also have no cause to intrude into the private realm, for example, into questions of faith, or to violate the individual's physical security. As already observed, the relationship between protection and obedience is central to Schmitt's thinking: So long as the sovereign is in the position to protect the subject, the latter is bound to obey. In this regard, too, Schmitt deserves to be called the Hobbes of the twentieth century.

I received assistance from a number of people in preparing this translation, including Carl Schmitt, who died in April 1985 in West Germany, three months shy of his ninety-seventh birthday. I am grateful to him and also to Ursula Ludz of Munich; Erna Hilfstein, Bernard Brown, and the late Edward Rosen of the Graduate Center of the City University of New York; G. L. Ulmen of New York; Thomas McCarthy, the series editor; and my assistants at the Graduate Center, Edwina McMahon and Jeffrey Kraus. Of course, the sole responsibility for the translation rests with me. I also wish to thank the Research Foundation of the City University of New York for a travel grant that enabled me to complete the research for this project.

This translation is dedicated to my wife Eleonora, to my sons Clarence, Claude, and Solan, and to the memory of Adrian.

26. Schmitt, "Starker Staat," pp. 91–92. See also Schmitt's "Grundrechte und Grundflichten" (1932), in *Verfassungsrechtliche Aufsätze aus den Jahren 1924–1954: Materialien zu einer Verfassungslehre*, 2d printing (Berlin, 1973), pp. 213–216; "Freiheitsrechte und institutionelle Garantien der Reichsverfassung" (1932), ibid., pp. 143–166; *Verfassungslehre*, 5th printing (Berlin, 1970), pp. 170–174; *Über die drei Arten des Rechtswissenschaftlichen Denkens* (Hamburg, 1934), pp. 56–57; Schwab, *The Challenge of the Exception*, pp. 115–125; and F. R. Cristi, "Hayek and Schmitt on the Rule of Law," *Canadian Journal of Political Science* 17/3 (September 1984): 529–532.

Preface to the Second Edition (1934)

The second edition of *Political Theology* remains unchanged. After twelve years, one can judge to what extent this short publication, which appeared in March 1922, has withstood the test of time. The disputes with liberal normativism and its kind of "constitutional state" are repeated verbatim. The few cuts that have been made involve passages that dealt with nonessentials.[1]

What has become clear in recent years are the numerous additional instances to which the idea of political theology is applicable. "Representation" from the fifteenth to the nineteenth century, the seventeenth-century monarchy, which is regarded as the god of baroque philosophy, the "neutral" power of the nineteenth century, "which reigned but did not rule," up to the conceptions of the pure measure and administrative state, "which

---

1. [Tr.] While it is true that the omissions in no way affect Schmitt's argument, they are interesting from another perspective, namely, the light they cast on Schmitt's relationship with Erich Kaufmann. Why, for example, did Schmitt omit the favorable references to this former friend, who was Jewish, while retaining positive references to the work of other Jews, notably Hans Kelsen?

administers but does not rule," are examples of the fruitfulness of the thought processes of political theology. The major problem concerning the individual stages of the process of secularization — from the theological stage by way of the metaphysical to the ethical and economic stages—was treated in my address "The Age of Neutralization and Depoliticization," delivered in Barcelona in October 1929.[2] Among Protestant theologians, Heinrich Forsthoff and Friedrich Gogarten, in particular, have shown that without a concept of secularization we cannot understand our history of the last centuries. To be sure, Protestant theology presents a different, supposedly unpolitical doctrine, conceiving of God as the "wholly other," just as in political liberalism the state and politics are conceived of as the "wholly other." We have come to recognize that the political is the total, and as a result we know that any decision about whether something is *unpolitical* is always a *political* decision, irrespective of who decides and what reasons are advanced. This also holds for the question whether a particular theology is a political or an unpolitical theology.

I would like to supplement my remarks on Hobbes concerning the two types of juristic thinking found at the end of the second chapter. This is vital because it concerns me professionally as a professor of law. I now distinguish not two but *three* types of legal thinking; in addition to the normativist and the decisionist types there is the institutional one. I have come to this conclusion as a result of discussions of my notion of "institutional guarantees" in German jurisprudence and my own studies of the profound

2. [Tr.] See Carl Schmitt, "Das Zeitalter der Neutralisierung und Entpolitisierung" (1929), in *Positionen und Begriffe im Kampf mit Weimar-Genf-Versailles, 1929–1939* (Hamburg, 1940), pp. 120–132.

and meaningful theory of institutions formulated by Maurice Hauriou.

Whereas the pure normativist thinks in terms of impersonal rules, and the decisionist implements the good law of the correctly recognized political situation by means of a personal decision, institutional legal thinking unfolds in institutions and organizations that transcend the personal sphere. And whereas the normativist in his distortion makes of law a mere mode of operation of a state bureaucracy, and the decisionist, focusing on the moment, always runs the risk of missing the stable content inherent in every great political movement, an isolated institutional thinking leads to the pluralism characteristic of a feudal-corporate growth that is devoid of sovereignty. The three spheres and elements of the political unity—state, movement, people[3]—thus may be joined to the three juristic types of thinking in their healthy as well as in their distorted forms. Not resting on natural right or the law of reason, merely attached to factually "valid" norms, the German theory of public law of the Wilhelmine and Weimar periods, with its so-called positivism and normativism, was only a deteriorated and therefore self-contradictory normativism. Blended with a specific kind of positivism, it was merely a degenerate decisionism, blind to the law, clinging to the "normative power of the factual" and not to a genuine decision. This formless mixture, unsuitable for any structure, was no match for any serious problem concerning state and constitution. This last epoch of German public law is characterized by the fact that the answer

---

3. [Tr.] *Staat, Bewegung, Volk: Die Dreigliederung der politischen Einheit* was Schmitt's first major treatise on the new order. Published in the fall of 1933, it offered an analysis of emerging constitutional realities in which Schmitt attempted to institutionalize a one-party state. See George Schwab, *The Challenge of the Exception: An. Introduction to the Political Ideas of Carl Schmitt between 1921 and 1936* (Berlin, 1970), pp. 108–113.

to one decisive case has remained outstanding, namely, the Prussian constitutional conflict with Bismarck; as a result we lack answers to all other decisive cases. To evade the necessary decision, German public law coined for such cases a saying that backfired and that it still carries as its motto: "Here is where public law stops."

Carl Schmitt
Berlin
November 1933

1

Definition of Sovereignty

Sovereign is he who decides on the exception.[1]

Only this definition can do justice to a borderline concept. Contrary to the imprecise terminology that is found in popular literature, a borderline concept is not a vague concept, but one pertaining to the outermost sphere. This definition of sovereignty must therefore be associated with a borderline case and not with routine. It will soon become clear that the exception is to be understood to refer to a general concept in the theory of the state, and not merely to a construct applied to any emergency decree or state of siege.

The assertion that the exception is truly appropriate for the juristic definition of sovereignty has a systematic, legal-logical

1. [Tr.] In the context of Schmitt's work, a state of exception includes any kind of severe economic or political disturbance that requires the application of extraordinary measures. Whereas an exception presupposes a constitutional order that provides guidelines on how to confront crises in order to reestablish order and stability, a state of emergency need not have an existing order as a reference point because *necessitas non habet legem*. See George Schwab, *The Challenge of the Exception* (Berlin, 1970), pp. 7, 42.

foundation. The decision on the exception is a decision in the true sense of the word. Because a general norm, as represented by an ordinary legal prescription, can never encompass a total exception, the decision that a real exception exists cannot therefore be entirely derived from this norm. When Robert von Mohl[2] said that the test of whether an emergency exists cannot be a juristic one, he assumed that a decision in the legal sense must be derived entirely from the content of a norm. But this is the question. In the general sense in which Mohl articulated his argument, his notion is only an expression of constitutional liberalism and fails to apprehend the independent meaning of the decision.

From a practical or a theoretical perspective, it really does not matter whether an abstract scheme advanced to define sovereignty (namely, that sovereignty is the highest power, not a derived power) is acceptable. About an abstract concept there will in general be no argument, least of all in the history of sovereignty. What is argued about is the concrete application, and that means who decides in a situation of conflict what constitutes the public interest or interest of the state, public safety and order, *le salut public*, and so on. The exception, which is not codified in the existing legal order, can at best be characterized as a case of extreme peril, a danger to the existence of the state, or the like. But it cannot be circumscribed factually and made to conform to a preformed law.

It is precisely the exception that makes relevant the subject of sovereignty, that is, the whole question of sovereignty. The precise details of an emergency cannot be anticipated, nor can one spell out what may take place in such a case, especially when

2. [Tr.] *Staatsrecht, Völkerrecht und Politik: Monographien*, vol. 2 (Tübingen, 1862), p. 626.

it is truly a matter of an extreme emergency and of how it is to be eliminated. The precondition as well as the content of jurisdictional competence in such a case must necessarily be unlimited. From the liberal constitutional point of view, there would be no jurisdictional competence at all. The most guidance the constitution can provide is to indicate who can act in such a case. If such action is not subject to controls, if it is not hampered in some way by checks and balances, as is the case in a liberal constitution, then it is clear who the sovereign is. He decides whether there is an extreme emergency as well as what must be done to eliminate it. Although he stands outside the normally valid legal system, he nevertheless belongs to it, for it is he who must decide whether the constitution needs to be suspended in its entirety.[3] All tendencies of modern constitutional development point toward eliminating the sovereign in this sense. The ideas of Hugo Krabbe and Hans Kelsen, which will be treated in the following chapter, are in line with this development. But whether the extreme exception can be banished from the world is not a juristic question. Whether one has confidence and hope that it can be eliminated depends on philosophical, especially on philosophical-historical or metaphysical, convictions.

There exist a number of historical presentations that deal with the development of the concept of sovereignty, but they are like textbook compilations of abstract formulas from which definitions of sovereignty can be extracted. Nobody seems to have taken the trouble to scrutinize the often-repeated but completely empty

---

3. [Tr.] As already noted in the introduction, Schmitt, in his study of dictatorship (*Die Diktatur*), considered the powers of the president to be commissarial in nature, that is, to be understood in the context of article 48. In the case of an exception the president could thus suspend the constitution but not abrogate it—an act characteristic of a sovereign form of dictatorship.

phraseology used to denote the highest power by the famous authors of the concept of sovereignty. That this concept relates to the critical case, the exception, was long ago recognized by Jean Bodin. He stands at the beginning of the modern theory of the state because of his work "Of the True Marks of Sovereignty" (chapter 10 of the first book of the *Republic*) rather than because of his often-cited definition ("sovereignty is the absolute and perpetual power of a republic"). He discussed his concept in the context of many practical examples, and he always returned to the question: To what extent is the sovereign bound to laws, and to what extent is he responsible to the estates? To this last, all-important question he replied that commitments are binding because they rest on natural law; but in emergencies the tie to general natural principles ceases. In general, according to him, the prince is duty bound toward the estates or the people only to the extent of fulfilling his promise in the interest of the people; he is not so bound under conditions of urgent necessity. These are by no means new theses. The decisive point about Bodin's concept is that by referring to the emergency, he reduced his analysis of the relationships between prince and estates to a simple either/or.

This is what is truly impressive in his definition of sovereignty; by considering sovereignty to be indivisible, he finally settled the question of power in the state. His scholarly accomplishment and the basis for his success thus reside in his having incorporated the decision into the concept of sovereignty. Today there is hardly any mention of the concept of sovereignty that does not contain the usual quotation from Bodin. But nowhere does one find cited the core quote from that chapter of the *Republic*. Bodin asked if the commitments of the prince to the estates or the people dissolve his sovereignty. He answered by referring to the case in which it becomes necessary to violate such commitments, to change laws or to suspend them entirely according to the requirements of a situation, a time, and a people. If in such cases the prince had to consult a senate or the people before he could act, he would have to be prepared to let his subjects dispense with him. Bodin considered this an absurdity because, according to him, the estates were not masters over the laws; they in turn would have to permit their prince to dispense with them. Sovereignty would thus become a play between two parties: Sometimes the people and sometimes the prince would rule, and that would be contrary to all reason and all law. Because the authority to suspend valid law—be it in general or in a specific case—is so much the actual mark of sovereignty, Bodin wanted to derive from this authority all other characteristics (declaring war and making peace, appointing civil servants, right of pardon, final appeal, and so on).

In contrast to traditional presentations, I have shown in my study of dictatorship that even the seventeenth-century authors of natural law understood the question of sovereignty to mean the question of the decision on the exception.[4] This is particularly true of Samuel von Pufendorf. Everyone agrees that whenever antagonisms appear within a state, every party wants the general good—therein resides after all the *bellum omnium contra omnes*. But sovereignty (and thus the state itself) resides in deciding this controversy, that is, in determining definitively what constitutes public order and security, in determining when they are disturbed, and so on. Public order and security manifest themselves very differently in reality, depending on whether a militaristic bu-

4. [Tr.] *Die Diktatur.*

reaucracy, a self-governing body controlled by the spirit of commercialism, or a radical party organization decides when there is order and security and when it is threatened or disturbed. After all, every legal order is based on a decision, and also the concept of the legal order, which is applied as something self-evident, contains within it the contrast of the two distinct elements of the juristic—norm and decision. Like every other order, the legal order rests on a decision and not on a norm.

Whether God alone is sovereign, that is, the one who acts as his acknowledged representative on earth, or the emperor, or prince, or the people, meaning those who identify themselves directly with the people, the question is always aimed at the subject of sovereignty, at the application of the concept to a concrete situation. Ever since the sixteenth century, jurists who discuss the question of sovereignty have derived their ideas from a catalogue of determining, decisive features of sovereignty that can in essence be traced to the points made by Bodin. To possess those powers meant to be sovereign. In the murky legal conditions of the old German Reich the argument on public law ran as follows: Because one of the many indications of sovereignty was undoubtedly present, the other dubious indications also had to be present. The controversy always centered on the question, Who assumes authority concerning those matters for which there are no positive stipulations, for example, a capitulation? In other words, Who is responsible for that for which competence has not been anticipated?

In a more familiar vein it was asked, Who is supposed to have unlimited power? Hence the discussion about the exception, the *extremus necessitatis casus*. This is repeated with the same legal-logical structure in the discussions on the so-called monarchical principle. Here, too, it is always asked who is entitled to decide those actions for which the constitution makes no provision; that is, who is competent to act when the legal system fails to answer the question of competence. The controversy concerning whether the individual German states were sovereign according to the constitution of 1871 was a matter of minor political significance. Nevertheless, the thrust of that argument can easily be recognized once more. The pivotal point of Max Seydel's attempt to prove that the individual states were sovereign had less to do with the question whether the remaining rights of the individual states were or were not subsumable than with the assertion that the competence of the Reich was circumscribed by the constitution, which in principle meant limited, whereas the competence of the individual states was in principle unlimited.

According to article 48 of the German constitution of 1919, the exception is declared by the president of the Reich but is under the control of parliament, the Reichstag, which can at any time demand its suspension. This provision corresponds to the development and practice of the liberal constitutional state, which attempts to repress the question of sovereignty by a division and mutual control of competences. But only the arrangement of the precondition that governs the invocation of exceptional powers corresponds to the liberal constitutional tendency, not the content of article 48. Article 48 grants unlimited power. If applied without check, it would grant exceptional powers in the same way as article 14 of the [French] Charter of 1815, which made the monarch sovereign. If the individual states no longer have the power to declare the exception, as the prevailing opinion on article 48 contends, then they no longer enjoy the status of states. Article

48 is the actual reference point for answering the question whether the individual German states are states.

If measures undertaken in an exception could be circumscribed by mutual control, by imposing a time limit, or finally, as in the liberal constitutional procedure governing a state of siege, by enumerating extraordinary powers, the question of sovereignty would then be considered less significant but would certainly not be eliminated. A jurisprudence concerned with ordinary day-to-day questions has practically no interest in the concept of sovereignty. Only the recognizable is its normal concern; everything else is a "disturbance." Such a jurisprudence confronts the extreme case disconcertedly, for not every extraordinary measure, not every police emergency measure or emergency decree, is necessarily an exception. What characterizes an exception is principally unlimited authority, which means the suspension of the entire existing order. In such a situation it is clear that the state remains, whereas law recedes. Because the exception is different from anarchy and chaos, order in the juristic sense still prevails even if it is not of the ordinary kind.

The existence of the state is undoubted proof of its superiority over the validity of the legal norm. The decision frees itself from all normative ties and becomes in the true sense absolute. The state suspends the law in the exception on the basis of its right of self-preservation, as one would say. The two elements of the concept *legal order* are then dissolved into independent notions and thereby testify to their conceptual independence. Unlike the normal situation, when the autonomous moment of the decision recedes to a minimum, the norm is destroyed in the exception. The exception remains, nevertheless, accessible to jurisprudence because both elements, the norm as well as the decision, remain within the framework of the juristic.

It would be a distortion of the schematic disjunction between sociology and jurisprudence if one were to say that the exception has no juristic significance and is therefore "sociology." The exception is that which cannot be subsumed; it defies general codification, but it simultaneously reveals a specifically juristic element—the decision in absolute purity. The exception appears in its absolute form when a situation in which legal prescriptions can be valid must first be brought about. Every general norm demands a normal, everyday frame of life to which it can be factually applied and which is subjected to its regulations. The norm requires a homogeneous medium. This effective normal situation is not a mere "superficial presupposition" that a jurist can ignore; that situation belongs precisely to its immanent validity. There exists no norm that is applicable to chaos. For a legal order to make sense, a normal situation must exist, and he is sovereign who definitely decides whether this normal situation actually exists.

All law is "situational law." The sovereign produces and guarantees the situation in its totality. He has the monopoly over this last decision. Therein resides the essence of the state's sovereignty, which must be juristically defined correctly, not as the monopoly to coerce or to rule, but as the monopoly to decide. The exception reveals most clearly the essence of the state's authority. The decision parts here from the legal norm, and (to formulate it paradoxically) authority proves that to produce law it need not be based on law.

The exception was something incommensurable to John Locke's doctrine of the constitutional state and the rationalist eighteenth century. The vivid awareness of the meaning of the exception that was reflected in the doctrine of natural law of the seventeenth century was soon lost in the eighteenth century, when a relatively lasting order was established. Emergency law was no law at all for Kant. The contemporary theory of the state reveals the interesting spectacle of the two tendencies facing one another, the rationalist tendency, which ignores the emergency, and the natural law tendency, which is interested in the emergency and emanates from an essentially different set of ideas. That a neo-Kantian like Kelsen does not know what to do with the exception is obvious. But it should be of interest to the rationalist that the legal system itself can anticipate the exception and can "suspend itself." That a norm or an order or a point of reference "establishes itself" appears plausible to the exponents of this kind of juristic rationalism. But how the systematic unity and order can suspend itself in a concrete case is difficult to construe, and yet it remains a juristic problem as long as the exception is distinguishable from a juristic chaos, from any kind of anarchy. The tendency of liberal constitutionalism to regulate the exception as precisely as possible means, after all, the attempt to spell out in detail the case in which law suspends itself. From where does the law obtain this force, and how is it logically possible that a norm is valid except for one concrete case that it cannot factually determine in any definitive manner?

It would be consequent rationalism to say that the exception proves nothing and that only the normal can be the object of scientific interest. The exception confounds the unity and order of the rationalist scheme. One encounters not infrequently a similar argument in the positive theory of the state. To the question of how to proceed in the absence of a budget law, Gerhard

Anschütz replied that this was not at all a legal question. "There is not only a gap in the law, that is, in the text of the constitution, but moreover in law as a whole, which can in no way be filled by juristic conceptual operations. Here is where public law stops."[5]

Precisely a philosophy of concrete life must not withdraw from the exception and the extreme case, but must be interested in it to the highest degree. The exception can be more important to it than the rule, not because of a romantic irony for the paradox, but because the seriousness of an insight goes deeper than the clear generalizations inferred from what ordinarily repeats itself. The exception is more interesting than the rule. The rule proves nothing; the exception proves everything: It confirms not only the rule but also its existence, which derives only from the exception. In the exception the power of real life breaks through the crust of a mechanism that has become torpid by repetition.

A Protestant theologian[6] who demonstrated the vital intensity possible in theological reflection in the nineteenth century stated: "The exception explains the general and itself. And if one wants to study the general correctly, one only needs to look around for a true exception. It reveals everything more clearly than does the general. Endless talk about the general becomes boring; there are exceptions. If they cannot be explained, then the general also cannot be explained. The difficulty is usually not noticed because the general is not thought about with passion but with a comfortable superficiality. The exception, on the other hand, thinks the general with intense passion."[7]

---

5. [Tr.] See Georg Meyer, *Lehrbuch des Deutschen Staatsrechts*, 7th ed., vol. 3, ed. G. Anschütz (Munich and Leipzig, 1919), p. 906.
6. [Tr.] The reference here is to Søren Kierkegaard.
7. [Tr.] The quote is from Kierkegaard's *Repetition*.

2

The Problem of Sovereignty as the Problem of the Legal Form and of the Decision

When theories and concepts of public law change under the impact of political events, the discussion is influenced for a time by the practical perspectives of the day. Traditional notions are modified to serve an immediate purpose. New realities can bring about a new sociological interest and a reaction against the "formalistic" method of treating problems of public law. But it is also possible for an effort to emerge that separates juristic treatment from changes in political conditions and achieves scientific objectivity precisely by a firm formal method of treatment. It is thus possible that this kind of political situation might produce various scientific tendencies and currents.

Of all juristic concepts the concept of sovereignty is the one most governed by actual interests. According to convention, the history of this concept begins with Bodin. But one cannot say that it has developed logically since the sixteenth century. The phases of its conceptual development are characterized by various political power struggles, not by a dialectical heightening inherent in the characteristics of the concept. Bodin's concept of sovereignty was derived in the sixteenth century from the final dissolution of Europe into national states and from the struggle of the absolute rulers with the estates. The self-consciousness of the newly created states was reflected in the eighteenth century in Vattel's concept of sovereignty, which was formulated within the context of international law. In the newly founded German Reich it became necessary after 1871 to advance a principle for distinguishing the authority of member states from the federal state. On the basis of this principle, the German theory of the state distinguishes between the concept of sovereignty and the concept of the state. What is gained by this distinction is that individual states may retain their status as states without being endowed with sovereignty. Nevertheless, the old definition, in phraseological variations, is always repeated: Sovereignty is the highest, legally independent, underived power.

Such a definition can be applied to the most different political-sociological configurations and can be enlisted to serve the most varied political interests. It is not the adequate expression of a reality but a formula, a sign, a signal. It is infinitely pliable, and therefore in practice, depending on the situation, either extremely useful or completely useless. It utilizes the superlative, "the highest power," to characterize a true quantity, even though from the standpoint of reality, which is governed by the law of causality, no single factor can be picked out and accorded such a superlative. In political reality there is no irresistible highest or greatest power that operates according to the certainty of natural law. Power proves nothing in law for the banal reason that Jean-Jacques Rousseau, in agreement with the spirit of his time, formulated as follows: Force is a physical power; the pistol that the robber holds is also a symbol of power.[1] The connection of actual power with the legally highest power is the fundamental problem of the concept of sovereignty. All the difficulties reside here. What is necessary is a definition that embraces this basic concept of jurisprudence. Such a definition cannot consist of general tautological predicates but rather must specify the essential juristic elements.

The most detailed treatment of the concept of sovereignty available in the past few years attempts a simple solution. This has been done by advancing a disjunction: sociology/jurisprudence, and with a simplistic either/or obtaining something purely sociological and something purely juristic. Kelsen followed this path in his *Das Problem der Souveränität und die Theorie des Völkerrechts*[2] and *Der soziologische und der juristische Staatsbegriff*.[3] To obtain in unadulterated purity a system of ascriptions to norms and a last uniform basic norm, all sociological elements have been left out of the juristic concept. The old contrast between *is* and *ought*, between causal and normative considerations, has been transferred to the contrast of sociology and jurisprudence, with greater emphasis and rigor than had already been done by Georg Jellinek and Kistiakowski, but with the same unproved certainty. The application of disjunctions emanating from another discipline or from epistemology appears to be the fate of jurisprudence. Using this procedure, Kelsen arrived at the unsurprising result that from the perspective of jurisprudence the state must be purely juristic, something normatively valid. It is not just any reality or any imagined entity alongside and outside the legal order. The state

1. *Du contrat social*, Bk. I, chap. 3.
2. Tübingen, 1920. [A second printing appeared in 1928.—tr.]
3. Tübingen, 1922. [A second printing appeared in 1928, and a third in Aalen in 1981.—tr.]

is nothing else than the legal order itself, which is conceived as a unity, to be sure. (That the problem resides precisely in this conception does not appear to create any difficulties.) The state is thus neither the creator nor the source of the legal order. According to Kelsen, all perceptions to the contrary are personifications and hypostatizations, duplications of the uniform and identical legal order in different subjects. The state, meaning the legal order, is a system of ascriptions to a last point of ascription and to a last basic norm. The hierarchical order that is legally valid in the state rests on the premise that authorizations and competences emanate from the uniform central point to the lowest point. The highest competence cannot be traceable to a person or to a sociopsychological power complex but only to the sovereign order in the unity of the system of norms. For juristic consideration there are neither real nor fictitious persons, only points of ascription. The state is the terminal point of ascription, the point at which the ascriptions, which constitute the essence of juristic consideration, "can stop." This "point" is simultaneously an "order that cannot be further derived." An uninterrupted system of orders, starting from the original, the ultimate, from the highest to a lower, meaning a delegated norm, can be conceived in such a fashion. The decisive argument, the one that is repeated and advanced against every intellectual opponent, remains the same: The basis for the validity of a norm can only be a norm; in juristic terms the state is therefore identical with its constitution, with the uniform basic norm.

The catchword of this deduction is *unity*. "The unity of the viewpoint of cognition demands peremptorily a monistic view." The dualism of the methods of sociology and jurisprudence ends in a monistic metaphysics. But the unity of the legal order, meaning the state, remains "purged" of everything sociological in the framework of the juristic. Is this juristic unity of the same kind as the worldwide unity of the entire system? How can it be possible to trace a host of positive attributes to a unity with the same point of ascription when what is meant is not the unity of a system of natural law or of a general theory of the law but the unity of a positive-valid order? Words such as *order, system,* and *unity* are only circumscriptions of the same postulate, which must demonstrate how it can be fulfilled in its purity. It has to be shown how a system can arise on the foundation of a "constitution" (which is either a further tautological circumscription of the "unity" or a brutal sociopolitical reality). The systematic unity is, according to Kelsen, an "independent act of juristic perception."

Let us for now disregard the interesting mathematical assumption that a point must be an order as well as a system and must also be identical with a norm; let us ask another question: On what does the intellectual necessity and objectivity of the various ascriptions with the various points of ascription rest if it does not rest on a positive determination, on a command? As if speaking time and again of uninterrupted unity and order would make them the most obvious things in the world; as if a fixed harmony existed between the result of free juristic knowledge and the complex that only in political reality constitutes a unity, what is discussed is a gradation of higher and lower orders supposedly found in everything that is attached to jurisprudence in the form of positive regulations.

The normative science to which Kelsen sought to elevate jurisprudence in all purity cannot be normative in the sense that the jurist by his own free will makes value assessments; he can only draw on the given (positively given) values. Objectivity thus appears to be possible, but has no necessary connection with positivity (*Positivität*). Although the values on which the jurist draws are given to him, he confronts them with relativistic superiority. He can construct a unity from everything in which he is interested juristically, provided he remains "pure." Unity and purity are easily attained when the basic difficulty is emphatically ignored and when, for formal reasons, everything that contradicts the system is excluded as impure. One who does not take any chances and remains resolutely methodological, not illustrating with even one concrete example how his jurisprudence differs from that which has been practiced until now as jurisprudence, finds it easy to be critical. Methodological conjuring, conceptual sharpening, and astute criticizing are only useful as preparatory work. If they do not come to the point when arguing that jurisprudence is something formal, they remain, despite all effort, in the antechamber of jurisprudence.

Kelsen solved the problem of the concept of sovereignty by negating it. The result of his deduction is that "the concept of sovereignty must be radically repressed."[4] This is in fact the old liberal negation of the state vis-à-vis law and the disregard of the independent problem of the realization of law. This conception has received a significant exposition by Hugo Krabbe. His theory of the sovereignty of laws rests on the thesis that it is not the state but law that is sovereign.[5] Kelsen appears to see in him only a precursor of his own doctrine identifying state and legal

---

4. *Das Problem der Souveränität*, p. 320.
5. His work on this subject was originally published in 1906; the enlarged edition appeared in 1919 under the title *Die moderne Staatsidee*. [English: *The Modern Idea of the State*, trans. George H. Sabine and Walter J. Shepard (New York and London, 1927).— tr.]

order. In fact, Krabbe's theory does share a common ideological root with Kelsen's result, but precisely where Kelsen was original, in his methodology, there is no connection between the exposition of the Dutch legal scholar and the epistemological and methodological distinctions of the German neo-Kantian. "Hòwever one wants to approach it, the doctrine of the sovereignty of law is," as Krabbe says, "either a record of what is already real or a postulate that ought to be realized."[6] The modern idea of the state, according to Krabbe, replaces personal force (of the king, of the authorities) with spiritual power. "We no longer live under the authority of persons, be they natural or artificial (legal) persons, but under the rule of laws, (spiritual) forces. This is the essence of the modern idea of the state." He continues, "These forces rule in the strictest sense of the word. Precisely because these forces emanate from the spiritual nature of man, they can be obeyed voluntarily." The basis, the source of the legal order, is "to be found only in men's feeling or sense of right." He concludes, "Nothing can be said further about this foundation: It is the only one that is real."

Even though Krabbe said he did not deal with sociological investigations into the forms of rule,[7] he did engage in essentially sociological explanations about the organizational formation of the modern state, in which the professional civil service, as an independent authority, identifies with the state, and in which the civil service status is represented as pertaining specifically to public law in contrast to the status of ordinary service. The distinction between public and private law is radically denied, insofar as it rests on a difference in the reality of subjects.[8] The further

6. *Die moderne Staatsidee*, 2d ed. (Haag, 1919), p. 39.
7. Ibid., p. 75.
8. Ibid., p. 138.

development of decentralization and self-government in all areas supposedly permits the modern idea of the state to emerge more and more clearly. It is not the state but law that is supposed to have power. "The old and oft-repeated view that power is the attribute of the state and the definition of the state as a manifestation of power can be conceded under the sole condition that this power is acknowledged as revealing itself in law and can have no effect except in issuing rules of law. What must be pointed out simultaneously is that the state reveals itself only in the making of law, be it by way of legislative enactment or by way of rewriting law. The state does not manifest itself in applying laws or in maintaining any sort of public interest whatever."[9] The only task of the state is to "make law," that is, to establish the legal value of interests.[10] "The concept of the state must not be defined by reference to the care of any specific interests whatever but solely by reference to the unique and original source of law from which all these interests and all other interests derive their legal value."[11]

The state is confined exclusively to producing law. But this does not mean that it produces the content of law. It does nothing but ascertain the legal value of interests as it springs from the people's feeling or sense of right. Therein resides a double limitation: first, a limitation on law, in contrast with interest or welfare, in short, with what is known in Kantian jurisprudence as "matter"; second, a limitation on the declaratory but by no means constitutive act of ascertaining. I will show that the problem of law as a substantial form lies precisely in this act of ascertaining. It must be observed that for Krabbe the contrast between law and

9. Ibid., p. 255.
10. Ibid., p. 261.
11. Ibid., p. 260.

interest is not the same as the contrast between form and matter. When he asserted that all public interests are subject to law, he meant that the legal interest is the highest in the modern state, the legal value the highest value.

Antagonism toward the centralized authoritarian state brought Krabbe close to the association theory. His fight against the authoritarian state is reminiscent of the well-known writings of Hugo Preuss. Otto von Gierke, the founder of association theory, formulated his notion of the state as follows: "The will of the state or the sovereign is not the final source of law but is the organ of the people convoked to express legal consciousness as it emerges from the life of the people."[12] The personal will of the ruler is spliced into the state as if into an organic whole. Yet law and state were for Gierke "equal powers," and he answered the basic question on their mutual relation by asserting that both are independent factors of human communal life, but one cannot be conceived of without the other, and neither exists before or through the other. In the instance of revolutionary constitutional changes there is a legal breach, a breach in legal continuity that can be ethically required or historically justified; but it remains a legal breach. As such, it can be repaired and can subsequently receive a legal justification "through some sort of legal procedure that will satisfy the legal consciousness of the people," for example, a constitutional agreement or a plebiscite or the sanctifying power of tradition.[13] There exists a tendency toward the reconciliation of law and power through which the otherwise unbearable "state

12. "Die Grundbegriffe des Staatsrechts und die neuesten Staatsrechtstheorien" (Part I), *Zeitschrift für die gesamte Staatswissenschaft* 30 (1974): 31. [It is possible that Schmitt worked with an offprint whose pagination did not coincide with the above. The quote is from part I and the page is 179.—tr.]
13. Ibid., p. 35. [p. 183—tr.]

of tension" can be eliminated. The equality of the state with the law is nevertheless veiled in Gierke because, according to him, the state's lawgiving is only "the last formal seal" the state stamps on the law; it is an "imprint of the state" that has only "external formal value." It is what Krabbe calls a mere ascertaining of the legal value, which does not belong to the character of law. This is why, according to Gierke, international law can be law even though it lacks state character. If the state is pushed into playing the role of a mere proclaiming herald, then it can no longer be sovereign. On the basis of Gierke's association theory, Preuss rejected the concept of sovereignty as a residue of the authoritarian state and discovered the community, based on associations and constituted from below, as an organization that did not need a monopoly on power and could thus also manage without sovereignty.

Among the newer representatives of association theory is Kurt Wolzendorff, who has tried to use the theory to solve "the problem of a new epoch of state." Among his numerous works,[14] his last is of the greatest interest here.[15] Its starting point is that the state needs law and law needs the state; but "law, as the deeper principle, holds the state in check in the final analysis." The state is the original power of rule, but it is so as the power of order, as the "form" of national life and not an arbitrary force applied by just any authority. What is demanded of this power is that it intervene only when the free individual or associational act proves to be insufficient; it should remain in the background as the *ultima ratio*. What is subject to order must not be coupled with economic, social, or cultural interests; these must be left to

14. *Deutsches Völkerrechtsdenken* (Munich, 1919); *Die Lüge des Völkerrechts* (Leipzig, 1919); *Geist des Staatsrechts* (Leipzig, 1920).
15. "Der reine Staat," *Zeitschrift für die gesamte Staatswissenschaft* 75 (1920): 199–229.

self-government. That a certain "maturity" belongs to self-government could, incidentally, make Wolzendorff's postulates dangerous, because in historical reality such historical-pedagogic problems often take an unexpected turn from discussion to dictatorship. Wolzendorff's pure state confines itself to maintaining order. To this state also belongs the formation of law, because all law is simultaneously a problem of the existence of the state order. The state should preserve law; it is "guardian, not master," guardian, not a mere "blind servant," and "responsible and ultimate guarantor." Wolzendorff sees in the idea of soviets an expression of this tendency to associational self-government, to confining the state to the "pure" function that belongs to it.

I don't believe that Wolzendorff was aware of how close he came with his "ultimate guarantor" to the authoritarian theory of the state, which is so completely antithetical to the associational and democratic conception of the state. This is why his last work, compared with those of Krabbe and other representatives of the association theory mentioned, is particularly important. It focuses the discussion on the decisive concept, namely, that of the form in its substantive sense. The authority of the order is valued so highly, and the function of guarantor is of such independence, that the state is no longer only the ascertainer or the "externally formal" transformer of the idea of law. The problem that arises is to what extent, with legal-logical necessity, every ascertainment and decision contains a constitutive element, an intrinsic value of form. Wolzendorff speaks of form as a "sociopsychological phenomenon," an active factor in historical-political life, the significance of which consists in giving opposing political forces an opportunity to grasp, in the conceptual structure of a state's constitution, a firm element of calculation.[16] The state thus becomes a form in the sense of a living formation. Wolzendorff did not distinguish clearly between a form that serves the purpose of calculable functioning and a form in the aesthetic sense, as the word is used, for example, by Hermann Hefele.

The confusion spreading in philosophy around the concept of form is repeated with especially disastrous results in sociology and jurisprudence. Legal form, technical form, aesthetic form, and finally the concept of form in transcendental philosophy denote essentially different things.

It is possible to distinguish three concepts of form in Max Weber's sociology of law. In one instance, the conceptual specification of the legal content whose legal form, the normative regulation, is as he says, but only as the "causal component of consensual acting." Then, when he speaks of differentiations in the categories of legal thought, he equates the word *formal* with the words *rationalized, professionally trained*, and, finally, *calculable*. He thus says that a formally developed law is a complex of conscious maxims of decisions, and what belongs to it sociologically is the participation of trained lawyers, representatives of the judiciary with civil service status, and others. Professional training, which means rational training, becomes necessary with the increased need for specialized knowledge. From this is derived the modern rationalization of law toward the specifically juristic and the development of "formal qualities."[17]

16. "Staatstheoretische Formen für politische Ideen," *Archiv des öffentlichen Rechts* 34 (1915): 477.
17. *Rechtssoziologie*, II, 1. [English: *Max Weber on Law in Economy and Society*, ed. Max Rheinstein (Cambridge, MA, 1966). This translation is mainly of Weber's "Rechtssoziologie" (Sociology of Law), which is a chapter of *Wirtschaft und Gesellschaft* (Economy and Society).—tr.]

Form can thus mean, first, the transcendental "condition" of juristic cognition; second, a regularity, an evenness, derived from repeated practice and professional reasoning. Because of its evenness and calculability, regularity passes over to the third form, the "rationalistic," that is, technical refinement, which, emerging from either the needs of specialized knowledge or the interests of a juristically educated bureaucracy, is oriented toward calculability and governed by the ideal of frictionless functioning.

We need not be detained here by the neo-Kantian conception of form. With regard to technical form, it means a specification governed by utility. Although it can be applied to the organized state apparatus, it does not touch the "judicial form." For example, the military command in its specification is in line with the technical ideal, not the legal one. That it can be aesthetically valued, perhaps even be made to lend itself to ceremonies, does not alter its technicity (*Technizität*). The age-old Aristotelian opposites of deliberation and action begin with two distinct forms; whereas deliberation is approachable through legal form, action is approachable only by a technical formation. The legal form is governed by the legal idea and by the necessity of applying a legal thought to a factual situation, which means that it is governed by the self-evolving law in the widest sense. Because the legal idea cannot realize itself, it needs a particular organization and form before it can be translated into reality. That holds true for the formation of a general legal norm into a positive law as well as for the application of a positive general legal norm by the judiciary or administration. A discussion of the peculiarity of the legal form must begin with this.

What significance can be given to the fact that in the contemporary theory of the state, neo-Kantian formalism has been thrown aside while, at the same time, a form is postulated from an entirely different direction? Is that another expression of those eternal mix-ups that are responsible for making the history of philosophy so monotonous? One thing is certain to be recognized in this modern theory of the state: The form should be transferred from the subjective to the objective. The concept of form in Emil Lask's theory of categories is still subjective, as it must necessarily be in every epistemologically critical approach. Kelsen contradicted himself when, on the one hand, he took such a critically derived subjectivist concept of form as the starting point and also conceived the unity of the legal order as an independent act of juristic perception, but then, on the other hand, when he professed his world view, demanded objectivity, and accused even Hegelian collectivism of a subjectivism of the state. The objectivity that he claimed for himself amounted to no more than avoiding everything personalistic and tracing the legal order back to the impersonal validity of an impersonal norm.

The multifarious theories of the concept of sovereignty—those of Krabbe, Preuss, Kelsen—demand such an objectivity. They agree that all personal elements must be eliminated from the concept of the state. For them, the personal and the command elements belong together. According to Kelsen, the conception of the personal right to command is the intrinsic error in the theory of state sovereignty; because the theory is premised on the subjectivism of command rather than on the objectively valid norm, he characterized the theory of the primacy of the state's legal order as "subjectivistic" and as a negation of the legal idea. In Krabbe the contrast between personal and impersonal was linked with the contrast between concrete and abstract, individual and general, which can be extended to the contrast between authority and legal prescription, authority and quality, and in its general philosophical formulation to the contrast between person and idea. Confronting in this fashion personal command with the impersonal validity of an abstract norm accords with the liberal constitutional tradition of the nineteenth century, which was lucidly and interestingly explained by Ahrens. For Preuss and Krabbe all conceptions of personality were aftereffects of absolute monarchy.

All these objections fail to recognize that the conception of personality and its connection with formal authority arose from a specific juristic interest, namely, an especially clear awareness of what the essence of the legal decision entails. Such a decision in the broadest sense belongs to every legal perception. Every legal thought brings a legal idea, which in its purity can never become reality, into another aggregate condition and adds an element that cannot be derived either from the content of the legal idea or from the content of a general positive legal norm that is to be applied. Every concrete juristic decision contains a moment of indifference from the perspective of content, because the juristic deduction is not traceable in the last detail to its premises and because the circumstance that requires a decision remains an independently determining moment. This has nothing to do with the causal and psychological origins of such a decision, even though the abstract decision as such is also of significance, but with the determination of the legal value. The certainty of the decision is, from the perspective of sociology, of particular interest in an age of intense commercial activity because in numerous cases commerce is less concerned with a particular content than with a calculable certainty. (So that I can accommodate myself accordingly, I am often less interested in how a timetable determines times of departure and arrival in a particular case than in its functioning reliably.) Legal communication offers an example of such a concern in the so-called formal strictness of the exchange law. The legal interest in the decision as such should not be mixed up with this kind of calculability. It is rooted in the character of the normative and is derived from the necessity of judging a concrete fact concretely even though what is given as a standard for the judgment is only a legal principle in its general universality. Thus a transformation takes place every time. That the legal idea cannot translate itself independently is evident from the fact that it says nothing about who should apply it. In every transformation there is present an *auctoritatis interpositio*. A distinctive determination of which individual person or which concrete body can assume such an authority cannot be derived from the mere legal quality of a maxim. This is the difficulty that Krabbe ignored.

That it is the instance of competence that renders a decision makes the decision relative, and in certain circumstances absolute and independent of the correctness of its content. This terminates any further discussion about whether there may still be some doubt. The decision becomes instantly independent of argumentative substantiation and receives an autonomous value. The entire theoretical and practical meaning of this is revealed in the theory of the faulty act of state. A legal validity is attributed to a wrong and faulty decision. The wrong decision contains a constitutive element precisely because of its falseness. But what is inherent in the idea of the decision is that there can never be absolutely declaratory decisions. That constitutive, specific element of a decision is, from the perspective of the content of the underlying norm, new and alien. Looked at normatively, the decision emanates from nothingness. The legal force of a decision is different from the result of substantiation. Ascription is not achieved with the aid of a norm; it happens the other way around. A point of ascription first determines what a norm is and what normative rightness is. A point of ascription cannot be derived from a norm, only a quality of a content. The formal in the specifically legal sense contrasts with this quality of content, not with the quantitative content of a causal connection. It should be understood that this last contrast is of no consequence to jurisprudence.

The peculiarity of the legal form must be recognized in its pure juristic nature. One should not speculate here about the philosophical meaning of the legal validity of a decision or about the motionlessness or the "eternity" of law, of law untouched by time and space, as did Adolf Merkl.[18] When Merkl said that "a development of the legal form is impossible because it dissolves the identity," he disclosed that he basically adheres to a roughly quantitative conception of form. But from this kind of form it is inexplicable how a personalistic element can appear in the doctrine of law and the state. This notion accords with the old constitutional tradition and its starting point that only a general legal prescription can be authoritative. The law gives authority, said Locke, and he consciously used the word *law* antithetically to *commissio*, which means the personal command of the monarch. But he did not recognize that the law does not designate to whom it gives authority. It cannot be just anybody who can execute and realize every desired legal prescription. The legal prescription, as the norm of decision, only designates how decisions should

18. *Archiv des öffentlichen Rechts* (1917): 19. [I have been unable to verify Schmitt's citation. It appears to me that what he had in mind was Adolf Merkl's "Die Rechtseinheit des österreichischen Staates," *Archiv des öffentlichen Rechts* 37 (1918), esp. 56–61.—tr.]

be made, not who should decide. In the absence of a pivotal authority, anybody can refer to the correctness of the content. But the pivotal authority is not derived from the norm of decision. Accordingly, the question is that of competence, a question that cannot be raised by and much less answered from the content of the legal quality of a maxim. To answer questions of competence by referring to the material is to assume that one's audience is a fool.

We can perhaps distinguish two types of juristic scientific thought according to whether an awareness of the normative character of the legal decision is or is not present. The classical representative of the decisionist type (if I may be permitted to coin this word) is Thomas Hobbes. The peculiar nature of this type explains why it, and not the other type, discovered the classic formulation of the antithesis: *autoritas, non veritas facit legem*.[19] The contrast of *autoritas* and *veritas* is more radical and precise than is Friedrich Julius Stahl's contrast: authority, not majority. Hobbes also advanced a decisive argument that connected this type of decisionism with personalism and rejected all attempts to substitute an abstractly valid order for a concrete sovereignty of the state. He discussed the demand that state power be subordinate to spiritual power because the latter is of a higher order. To this reasoning he replied that if one "power" (*potestas*) were to be subordinate to another, the meaning would be nothing more than that the one who possesses power is subordinate to the other who possesses power: "He which hath the one Power is subject to him that hath the other." To speak of superior and inferior and attempt to remain simultaneously abstract is to him incomprehensible ("we cannot understand"). "For Subjection,

19. *Leviathan*, chap. 26.

Command, Right and Power are accidents not of Powers but of Persons."[20] He illustrated this with one of those comparisons that in the unmistakable soberness of his healthy common sense, he knew how to apply so strikingly: Power or order can be subordinate to another just as the art of the saddler is subordinate to that of the rider; but the important thing is that despite this abstract ladder of orders, no one thinks of subordinating the individual saddler to every single rider and obligating him to obey.

It is striking that one of the most consequential representatives of this abstract scientific orientation of the seventeenth century became so personalistic. This is because as a juristic thinker he wanted to grasp the reality of societal life just as much as he, as a philosopher and natural scientist, wanted to grasp the reality of nature. He did not discover that there is a juristic reality and life that need not be reality in the sense of the natural sciences. Mathematical relativism and nominalism also operate concurrently. Often he seemed to be able to construct the unity of the state from any arbitrary given point. But juristic thought in those days had not yet become so overpowered by the natural sciences that he, in the intensity of his scientific approach, should unsuspectingly have overlooked the specific reality of legal life inherent in the legal form. The form that he sought lies in the concrete decision, one that emanates from a particular authority. In the independent meaning of the decision, the subject of the decision has an independent meaning, apart from the question of content. What matters for the reality of legal life is who decides. Alongside the question of substantive correctness stands the question of competence. In the contrast between the subject and

20. Ibid., chap. 42.

the content of a decision and in the proper meaning of the subject lies the problem of the juristic form. It does not have the a priori emptiness of the transcendental form because it arises precisely from the juristically concrete. The juristic form is also not the form of technical precision because the latter has a goal-oriented interest that is essentially material and impersonal. Finally, it is also not the form of aesthetic production, because the latter knows no decision.

3

Political Theology

All significant concepts of the modern theory of the state are secularized theological concepts not only because of their historical development—in which they were transferred from theology to the theory of the state, whereby, for example, the omnipotent God became the omnipotent lawgiver—but also because of their systematic structure, the recognition of which is necessary for a sociological consideration of these concepts. The exception in jurisprudence is analogous to the miracle in theology. Only by being aware of this analogy can we appreciate the manner in which the philosophical ideas of the state developed in the last centuries.

The idea of the modern constitutional state triumphed together with deism, a theology and metaphysics that banished the miracle from the world. This theology and metaphysics rejected not only the transgression of the laws of nature through an exception brought about by direct intervention, as is found in the idea of a miracle, but also the sovereign's direct intervention in a valid legal order. The rationalism of the Enlightenment rejected the exception in every form. Conservative authors of the counter-revolution who were theists could thus attempt to support the personal sovereignty of the monarch ideologically, with the aid of analogies from a theistic theology.

I have for a long time referred to the significance of such fundamentally systematic and methodical analogies.[1] A detailed presentation of the meaning of the concept of the miracle in this context will have to be left to another time. What is relevant here is only the extent to which this connection is appropriate for a sociology of juristic concepts. The most interesting political application of such analogies is found in the Catholic philosophers of the counterrevolution, in Bonald, de Maistre, and Donoso Cortés. What we immediately recognize in them is a conceptually clear and systematic analogy, and not merely that kind of playing with ideas, whether mystical, natural-philosophical, or even romantic, which, as with everything else, so also with state and society, yields colorful symbols and pictures.

The clearest philosophical expression of that analogy is found in Leibniz.[2] Emphasizing the systematic relationship between jurisprudence and theology, he rejected a comparison of jurisprudence with medicine and mathematics: "We have deservedly transferred the model of our division from theology to jurisprudence because the similarity of these two disciplines is astonishing." Both have a double principle, reason (hence there is

---

1. *Der Wert des Staates* (Tübingen, 1914); *Politische Romantik* (Munich and Leipzig, 1919); *Die Diktatur: Von den Anfängen des modernen Souveränitätsgedankens bis zum proletarischen Klassenkampf* (Munich and Leipzig, 1921). [A second edition of *Politische Romantik* appeared in 1925; on the various editions of *Die Diktatur*, see the introduction, note 15.—tr.]
2. *Nova Methodus*, paras. 4, 5.

a natural theology and a natural jurisprudence) and scripture, which means a book with positive revelations and directives.

Adolf Menzel noted in an essay[3] that today sociology has assumed functions that were exercised in the seventeenth and eighteenth centuries by natural law, namely, to utter demands for justice and to enunciate philosophical-historical constructions or ideals. He seems to believe that sociology is inferior to jurisprudence, which is supposed to have become positive. He attempts to show that all heretofore sociological systems end up by making "political tendencies appear scientific." But whoever takes the trouble of examining the public law literature of positive jurisprudence for its basic concepts and arguments will see that the state intervenes everywhere. At times it does so as a *deus ex machina*, to decide according to positive statute a controversy that the independent act of juristic perception failed to bring to a generally plausible solution; at other times it does so as the graceful and merciful lord who proves by pardons and amnesties his supremacy over his own laws. There always exists the same inexplicable identity: lawgiver, executive power, police, pardoner, welfare institution. Thus to an observer who takes the trouble to look at the total picture of contemporary jurisprudence, there appears a huge cloak-and-dagger drama, in which the state acts in many disguises but always as the same invisible person. The "omnipotence" of the modern lawgiver, of which one reads in every textbook on public law, is not only linguistically derived from theology.

Many reminiscences of theology also appear in the details of the argumentation, most of course with polemical intent. In a positivistic age it is easy to reproach an intellectual opponent

3. *Naturrecht und Soziologie* (Vienna and Leipzig, 1912).

with the charge of indulging in theology or metaphysics. If the reproach were intended as more than mere insult, at least the following question could suggest itself: What is the source of this inclination for such theological and metaphysical derailments? One would have had to investigate whether they may be explained historically, perhaps as an aftereffect of monarchical public law, which identified the theistic God with the king, or whether they are underpinned by systematic or methodical necessities. I readily admit that because of an inability to master intellectually contradictory arguments or objections, some jurists introduce the state in their works by a mental short circuit, just as certain metaphysicians misuse the name of God. But this does not yet resolve the substantive problem.

Until now one was generally satisfied with casual intimations only. In his publication on the law in the formal and material sense, Albert Hänel[4] raised the old objection that it is "metaphysics" to demand, for the sake of the uniformity and reliability of the state's will (both of which he thus does not deny), the concentration of all functions of the state in one organ. Hugo Preuss[5] too attempted to defend his association concept of the state by relegating his opponents to theology and metaphysics. The concept of sovereignty in the theory of the state by Laband and Jellinek and the theory of the "sole supremacy of the state" make the state an abstract person so to speak, a *unicum sui generis*, with a monopoly of power "mystically produced." To Preuss this was a legal disguise of the theory of the divine right of kings, a repetition of the teachings of Maurenbrecher with the modification that the religious fiction is replaced by the juristic fiction. Thus

---

4. *Das Gesetz im Formellen und Materiellen Sinne* (Leipzig, 1888), p. 150. [2d printing (Darmstadt, 1968)—tr.]
5. *Festgabe für Laband*, vol. 2 (1908), p. 236. [I was unable to verify this citation—tr.]

Preuss, a representative of the organic theory of the state, re-
proached his opponent for theologizing. In his critical studies of
the concept of the juristic person, Bernatzik[6] maintained, on the
other hand, that it is precisely the organic doctrine of the state
that is theology. Bernatzik attempted to destroy the organic ideas
of Stein, Schulze, Gierke, and Preuss with the sneering remark
that if the organs of the collective legal person should once again
be persons, then every administrative authority, every court, and
so on, would be a juristic person and the state in its entirety
would also once again be such a sole juristic person. "The attempt
to comprehend the dogma of the Trinity would, by comparison,
be an easy matter." He also dismissed Stobbes's opinion that
the entire collective personality is a legal person with the sentence
that he does not understand "twists like this one that are reminiscent of the dogma of the Trinity." Yet he himself said, "It
already resides in the concept of legal competence that its source,
the state's legal order, must posit itself as the subject of all law,
consequently as a juristic person." This process of positing itself
was apparently so simple and plausible to Bernatzik that he mentioned a deviating opinion as representing "only a curiosity."
Nevertheless, he did not ask himself why there is a greater logical
necessity for the source of legal competence, namely, the legal
order, that is, the state's legal order, to posit itself as a product
than there is for Stahl's dictum that only a person can be the
basis for another person.

Kelsen has the merit of having stressed since 1920 the methodical relationship of theology and jurisprudence. In his last

---

6. "Kritische Studien über den Begriff der juristischen Person und über die juristische
Persönlichkeit der Behörden insbesondere," *Archiv des öffentlichen Rechts* 5 (1890): 210,
225, 244.

work on the sociological and the juristic concepts of the state[7] he introduced many analogies. Although diffuse, these analogies make it possible for those with a deeper understanding of the history of ideas to discern the inner heterogeneity between his neo-Kantian epistemological point of departure and his ideological and democratic results. At the foundation of his identification of state and legal order rests a metaphysics that identifies the lawfulness of nature and normative lawfulness. This pattern of thinking is characteristic of the natural sciences. It is based on the rejection of all "arbitrariness," and attempts to banish from the realm of the human mind every exception. In the history of the parallel of theology and jurisprudence, such a conviction finds its place most appropriately probably in J. S. Mill. In the interest of objectivity and because of his fear of arbitrariness, he too emphasized the validity without exception of every kind of law. But he probably did not assume, as did Kelsen, that the free deed of legal perception could shape just any mass of positive laws into the cosmos of its system, because this would nullify the objectivity already achieved. For a metaphysics that suddenly falls into the pathos of objectivity, it should make no difference whether an unconditional positivism directly adheres to the law that presents itself, or whether it bothers to first establish a system.

Kelsen, as soon as he goes one step beyond his methodological criticism, operates with a concept of causation that is entirely natural-scientific. This is most clearly demonstrated by his belief that Hume's and Kant's critique of the concept of substance can be transferred to the theory of the state.[8] But he fails thereby

7. [Tr.] *Der Soziologische und der juristische Staatsbegriff* (Tübingen, 1922).
8. Ibid, p. 208.

to see that the concept of substance in Scholastic thought is entirely different from that in mathematical and natural-scientific thinking. The distinction between the substance and the practice of law, which is of fundamental significance in the history of the concept of sovereignty,[9] cannot be grasped with concepts rooted in the natural sciences and yet is an essential element of legal argumentation. When Kelsen gives the reasons for opting for democracy, he openly reveals the mathematical and natural-scientific character of his thinking:[10] Democracy is the expression of a political relativism and a scientific orientation that are liberated from miracles and dogmas and based on human understanding and critical doubt.

For the sociology of the concept of sovereignty it is altogether vital to be clear about the sociology of legal concepts as such. The aforementioned systematic analogy between theological and juristic concepts is stressed here precisely because a sociology of legal concepts presupposes a consistent and radical ideology.[11] Yet it would be erroneous to believe that therein resides a spiritualist philosophy of history as opposed to a materialist one.

The political theology of the Restoration offers an exemplary illustration of the sentence Max Weber articulated in his critique of Rudolf Stammler's philosophy of right, namely, that it is possible to confront irrefutably a radical materialist philosophy of history with a similarly radical spiritualist philosophy of history. The authors of the counterrevolution explained political change as a result of change in outlook and traced the French Revolution to the philosophy of the Enlightenment. It was nothing more than

9. *Die Diktatur*, pp. 44, 105, 194.
10. "Vom Wesen und Wert der Demokratie," *Archiv für Sozialwissenschaft und Sozialpolitik* 47 (1920–21): 84.
11. [Tr.] Schmitt uses the word *radical* here in the sense of "thought out to the end."

a clear antithesis when radical revolutionaries conversely attributed a change in thought to a change in the political and social conditions. That religious, philosophical, artistic, and literary changes are closely linked with political and social conditions was already a widespread dogma in western Europe, especially in France, in the 1820s.

In the Marxist philosophy of history this interdependence is radicalized to an economic dependence; it is given a systematic basis by seeking a point of ascription also for political and social changes and by finding it in the economic sphere. This materialist explanation makes a separate consideration of ideology impossible, because everywhere it sees only "reflexes," "reflections," and "disguises" of economic relations. Consequently, it looks with suspicion at psychological explanations and interpretations, at least in their vulgar form. Precisely because of its massive rationalism, this philosophy can easily turn into an irrationalist conception of history, since it conceives all thought as being a function and an emanation of vital processes. The anarchic-syndicalist socialism of Georges Sorel thus linked in this fashion Henri Bergson's philosophy of life with Marx's economic conception of history.

Both the spiritualist explanation of material processes and the materialist explanation of spiritual phenomena seek causal relations. At first they construct a contrast between two spheres, and then they dissolve this contrast into nothing by reducing one to the other. This method must necessarily culminate in a caricature. Just as Engels saw the Calvinist dogma of predestination as a reflection of capitalist competition in terms of its senselessness and incalculability, it would be just as easy to reduce the modern theory of relativity and its success to currency relations in today's world market, and thus to find the economic basis of that theory. Some would call such a procedure the sociology of a concept or a theory. This, however, is of no concern to us.

It is otherwise with the sociological method, which, with a view to certain ideas and intellectual constructions, seeks the typical group of persons who arrive at certain ideological results from the peculiarity of their sociological situations. In this sense one can speak of a sociology of juristic concepts, in the case of Max Weber, who traced the differentiation of the various legal fields to the development of trained jurists, civil servants who administer justice, or legal dignitaries.[12] The sociological "peculiarity of the group of persons who professionally concern themselves with forming law" necessitates definite methods and views of juristic thinking. But this is still not a sociology of a legal concept.

To trace a conceptual result back to a sociological carrier is psychology; it involves the determination of a certain kind of motivation of human action. This is a sociological problem, but not a problem of the sociology of a concept. If this method is applied to intellectual accomplishments, it leads to explanations in terms of the milieu, or even to the ingenious "psychology" that is known as the sociology of specific types, that is, of the bureaucrat, the attorney, or the professor who is employed by the state. The Hegelian system, for example, if investigated by applying this method, would have to be characterized as the philosophy of the professional lecturer, who by his economic and social situation is enabled to become, with contemplative superiority, aware of absolute consciousness, which means to practice his profession as a lecturer of philosophy; or it would be

12. *Rechtssoziologie*, II, 1.

possible to view Kelsen's jurisprudence as the ideology of the lawyer-bureaucrat practicing in changing political circumstances, who, under the most diverse forms of authority and with a relativistic superiority over the momentary political authority, seeks to order systematically the positive decrees and regulations that are handed down to him. In its consequent manner this type of sociology is best assigned to belles-lettres; it provides a socio-psychological "portrait" produced by a method that cannot be distinguished from the brilliant literary criticism of a Sainte-Beuve, for example.

Altogether different is the sociology of concepts, which is advanced here and alone has the possibility of achieving a scientific result for a concept such as sovereignty. This sociology of concepts transcends juridical conceptualization oriented to immediate practical interest. It aims to discover the basic, radically systematic structure and to compare this conceptual structure with the conceptually represented social structure of a certain epoch. There is no question here of whether the idealities produced by radical conceptualization are a reflex of sociological reality, or whether social reality is conceived of as the result of a particular kind of thinking and therefore also of acting. Rather this sociology of concepts is concerned with establishing proof of two spiritual but at the same time substantial identities. It is thus not a sociology of the concept of sovereignty when, for example, the monarchy of the seventeenth century is characterized as the real that is "mirrored" in the Cartesian concept of God. But it is a sociology of the concept of sovereignty when the historical-political status of the monarchy of that epoch is shown to correspond to the general state of consciousness that was characteristic of western Europeans at that time, and when the juristic construction of the historical-political reality can find a concept whose structure is in accord with the structure of metaphysical concepts. Monarchy thus becomes as self-evident in the consciousness of that period as democracy does in a later epoch.

The presupposition of this kind of sociology of juristic concepts is thus a radical conceptualization, a consistent thinking that is pushed into metaphysics and theology. The metaphysical image that a definite epoch forges of the world has the same structure as what the world immediately understands to be appropriate as a form of its political organization. The determination of such an identity is the sociology of the concept of sovereignty. It proves that in fact, as Edward Caird said in his book on Auguste Comte, metaphysics is the most intensive and the clearest expression of an epoch.

"Imitate the immutable decrees of the divinity." This was the ideal of the legal life of the state that was immediately evident to the rationalism of the eighteenth century. This utterance is found in Rousseau's essay *Political Economy*. The politicization of theological concepts, especially with respect to the concept of sovereignty, is so striking that it has not escaped any true expert on his writings. Said Emile Boutmy, "Rousseau applies to the sovereign the idea that the philosophes hold of God: He may do anything that he wills but he may not will evil."[13] In the theory of the state of the seventeenth century, the monarch is identified with God and has in the state a position exactly analogous to that attributed to God in the Cartesian system of the world. According to Atger, "The prince develops all the inherent

13. "La declaration des droits de l'homme et du citoyen et M. Jellinek," *Annales des sciences politiques* 4 (1902): 418.

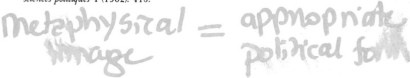

"spirit of " Mot umhter urber" [handwritten annotation]

characteristics of the state by a sort of continual creation. The prince is the Cartesian god transposed to the political world."[14]

There is psychologically (and, from the point of view of a phenomenologist, phenomenologically as well) a complete identity. A continuous thread runs through the metaphysical, political, and sociological conceptions that postulate the sovereign as a personal unit and primeval creator. The fine tale of the *Discours de la méthode* provides an extraordinarily instructive example. It is a document of the new rationalist spirit. In the depth of doubt, it finds consolation by using reason unswervingly: "J'étais assuré d'user en tout de ma raison." But what is it that becomes clear in the first place to the mind suddenly forced to reason? That the works created by several masters are not as perfect as those created by one. "One sole architect" must construct a house and a town; the best constitutions are those that are the work of a sole wise legislator, they are "devised by only one"; and finally, a sole God governs the world. As Descartes once wrote to Mersenne, "It is God who established these laws in nature just as a king establishes laws in his kingdom."

The seventeenth and eighteenth centuries were dominated by this idea of the sole sovereign, which is one of the reasons why, in addition to the decisionist cast of his thinking, Hobbes remained personalistic and postulated an ultimate concrete deciding instance, and why he also heightened his state, the Leviathan, into an immense person and thus point-blank straight into mythology. This he did despite his nominalism and natural-scientific approach and his reduction of the individual to the atom. For him this was no anthropomorphism—from which he was truly free—but a methodical and systematic postulate of his juristic thinking. But

14. *Essai sur l'histoire des doctrines du contrat social* (1906), p. 136.

the image of the architect and master builder of the world reflects a confusion that is characteristic of the concept of causality. The world architect is simultaneously the creator and the legislator, which means the legitimizing authority. Throughout the Enlightenment period until the French Revolution, such an architect of world and state was called the legislator.

Since then the consistency of exclusively scientific thinking has also permeated political ideas, repressing the essentially juristic-ethical thinking that had predominated in the age of the Enlightenment. The general validity of a legal prescription has become identified with the lawfulness of nature, which applies without exception. The sovereign, who in the deistic view of the world, even if conceived as residing outside the world, had remained the engineer of the great machine, has been radically pushed aside. The machine now runs by itself. The metaphysical proposition that God enunciates only general and not particular declarations of will governed the metaphysics of Leibniz and Nicolas Malebranche. The general will of Rousseau became identical with the will of the sovereign; but simultaneously the concept of the general also contained a quantitative determination with regard to its subject, which means that the people became the sovereign. The decisionistic and personalistic element in the concept of sovereignty was thus lost. The will of the people is always good: "The people are always virtuous." Said Emmanuel Sieyès, "In whatever manner a nation expresses its wishes, it is enough that it wishes; all forms are good but its will is always the supreme law."

But the necessity by which the people always will what is right is not identical with the rightness that emanated from the commands of the personal sovereign. In the struggle of opposing interests and coalitions, absolute monarchy made the decision and thereby created the unity of the state. The unity that a people represents does not possess this decisionist character; it is an organic unity, and with national consciousness the ideas of the state originated as an organic whole. The theistic as well as the deistic concepts of God become thus unintelligible for political metaphysics.

It is true, nevertheless, that for some time the aftereffects of the idea of God remained recognizable. In America this manifested itself in the reasonable and pragmatic belief that the voice of the people is the voice of God—a belief that is at the foundation of Jefferson's victory of 1801. Tocqueville in his account of American democracy observed that in democratic thought the people hover above the entire political life of the state, just as God does above the world, as the cause and the end of all things, as the point from which everything emanates and to which everything returns. Today, on the contrary, such a well-known legal and political philosopher of the state as Kelsen can conceive of democracy as the expression of a relativistic and impersonal scientism. This notion is in accord with the development of political theology and metaphysics in the nineteenth century.

To the conception of God in the seventeenth and eighteenth centuries belongs the idea of his transcendence vis-à-vis the world, just as to that period's philosophy of state belongs the notion of the transcendence of the sovereign vis-à-vis the state. Everything in the nineteenth century was increasingly governed by conceptions of immanence. All the identities that recur in the political ideas and in the state doctrines of the nineteenth century rest on such conceptions of immanence: the democratic thesis of the identity of the ruler and the ruled, the organic theory of the

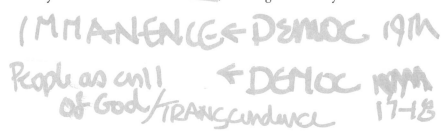

state with the identity of the state and sovereignty, the constitutional theory of Krabbe with the identity of sovereignty and the legal order, and finally Kelsen's theory of the identity of the state and the legal order.

After the writers of the Restoration developed a political theology, the radicals who opposed all existing order directed, with heightened awareness, their ideological efforts against the belief in God altogether, fighting that belief as if it were the most fundamental expression of the belief in any authority and unity. The battle against God was taken up by Proudhon under the clear influence of Auguste Comte. Bakunin continued it with Scythian fury. The battle against traditional religiosity can be traced naturally to many different political and sociological motives: the conservative posture of ecclesiastical Christianity, the alliance of throne and altar, the number of prominent authors who were "déclassé," the appearance of an art and literature in the nineteenth century whose genial representatives, at least in the decisive periods of their lives, had been spat out by the bourgeois order—all this is still largely unrecognized and unappreciated in its sociological detail.

The main line of development will undoubtedly unfold as follows: Conceptions of transcendence will no longer be credible to most educated people, who will settle for either a more or less clear immanence-pantheism or a positivist indifference toward any metaphysics. Insofar as it retains the concept of God, the immanence philosophy, which found its greatest systematic architect in Hegel, draws God into the world and permits law and the state to emanate from the immanence of the objective. But among the most extreme radicals, a consequent atheism began to prevail. The German left-Hegelians were most conscious of this tendency. They were no less vehement than Proudhon in proclaiming that mankind had to be substituted for God. Marx and Engels never failed to recognize that this ideal of an unfolding self-conscious mankind must end in anarchic freedom. Precisely because of his youthful intuition, the utterance of the young Engels in the years 1842–1844 is of the greatest significance: "The essence of the state, as that of religion, is mankind's fear of itself."[15]

If viewed from this perspective of the history of ideas, the development of the nineteenth-century theory of the state displays two characteristic moments: the elimination of all theistic and transcendental conceptions and the formation of a new concept of legitimacy. The traditional principle of legitimacy obviously lost all validity. Neither the version of the Restoration based on private law and patrimony nor the one founded on a sentimental and reverent attachment was able to resist this development. Since 1848 the theory of public law has become "positive," and behind this word is usually hidden its dilemma; or the theory has propounded in different paraphrases the idea that all power resides in the *pouvoir constituant* of the people, which means that the democratic notion of legitimacy has replaced the monarchical. It was therefore an occurrence of utmost significance that Donoso Cortés, one of the foremost representatives of decisionist thinking and a Catholic philosopher of the state, one who was intensely conscious of the metaphysical kernel of all politics, concluded in reference to the revolution of 1848, that the epoch of royalism was at an end. Royalism is no longer because there are no kings. Therefore legitimacy no longer exists in the traditional sense.

15. Friedrich Engels, *Schriften aus der Frühzeit*, ed. G. Mayer (Berlin, 1920), p. 281.

For him there was thus only one solution: dictatorship. It is the solution that Hobbes also reached by the same kind of decisionist thinking, though mixed with mathematical relativism. *Autoritas, non veritas facit legem.*

A detailed presentation of this kind of decisionism and a thorough appreciation of Donoso Cortés are not yet available. Here it can only be pointed out that the theological mode of thought of the Spaniard was in complete accord with the thought of the Middle Ages, whose construction was juristic. All his perceptions, all his arguments, down to the last atom, were juristic; his lack of understanding of the mathematical natural-scientific thinking of the nineteenth century mirrored the outlook of natural-scientific thinking toward decisionism and the specific logic of the juristic thinking that culminates in a personal decision.

4

On the Counterrevolutionary Philosophy of the State (de Maistre, Bonald, Donoso Cortés)

German romantics possess an odd trait: everlasting conversation. Novalis and Adam Müller feel at home with it; to them it constitutes the true realization of their spirits. Catholic political philosophers such as de Maistre, Bonald, and Donoso Cortés—who are called romantics in Germany because they were conservative or reactionary and idealized the conditions of the Middle Ages—would have considered everlasting conversation a product of a gruesomely comic fantasy, for what characterized their counterrevolutionary political philosophy was the recognition that their times needed a decision. And with an energy that rose to an extreme between the two revolutions of 1789 and 1848, they thrust the notion of the decision to the center of their thinking. Wherever Catholic philosophy of the nineteenth century was engaged, it expressed the idea in one form or another that there was now a great alternative that no longer allowed of synthesis. No medium exists, said Cardinal Newman, between catholicity and atheism. Everyone formulated a big either/or, the rigor of which sounded more like dictatorship than everlasting conversation.

The Restoration fought the activist spirit of the French Revolution with ideas such as tradition and custom and with the belief that history progresses slowly. Ideas of that sort could have led to a complete negation of natural reason and to an absolute moralistic passivity that would have considered becoming active altogether evil. Traditionalism had been theologically refuted by J. Lupus and P. Chastel, by the latter, incidentally, with references to the *sentimentalisme allemand* that was supposed to be the source of such errors. In the final analysis, extreme traditionalism actually meant an irrational rejection of every intellectually conscious decision, even though Bonald, the founder of traditionalism, was far removed from the idea of an everlasting evolution spurred in and of itself. But his intellect had an altogether different structure from that of de Maistre or even that of Donoso Cortés. Bonald often showed himself to be surprisingly German. But his belief in tradition never turned into something like Schelling's philosophy of nature, Adam Müller's mixture of opposites, or Hegel's belief in history. For Bonald tradition offered the sole possibility of gaining the content that man was capable of accepting metaphysically, because the intellect of the individual was considered too weak and wretched to be able to recognize truth by itself. What a contrast there is to each of those three Germans in the horrifying picture that depicts the course of humanity in history: a herd of blind men led by a blind man, who gropes his way forward with a cane! The antitheses and distinctions that Bonald was so fond of and that earned him the name of a Scholastic contain in truth moral disjunctions—and not polarities in the sense of Schelling's philosophy of nature, which reveal "indifference points," or mere dialectical negations of the historical process. "I find myself constantly between two abysses, I walk always between being and nothingness." Such moral disjunctions represent contrasts between good and evil, God and the devil; between them an either/or exists in the sense of a life-and-death struggle that does not recognize a synthesis and a "higher third."

De Maistre spoke with particular fondness of sovereignty, which essentially meant decision. To him the relevance of the state rested on the fact that it provided a decision, the relevance of the Church on its rendering of the last decision that could not be appealed. Infallibility was for him the essence of the decision that cannot be appealed, and the infallibility of the spiritual order was of the same nature as the sovereignty of the state order. The two words *infallibility* and *sovereignty* were "perfectly synonymous."[1] To him, every sovereignty acted as if it were infallible, every government was absolute—a sentence that an anarchist could pronounce verbatim, even if his intention was an entirely different one. In this sentence there lies the clearest antithesis in the entire history of political ideas. All the anarchist theories from Babeuf to Bakunin, Kropotkin, and Otto Gross revolve around the one axiom: "The people are good, but the magistrate is corruptible." De Maistre asserted the exact opposite, namely, that authority as such is good once it exists: "Any government is good once it is established," the reason being that a decision is inherent in the mere existence of a governmental authority, and the decision as such is in turn valuable precisely because, as far as the most essential issues are concerned, making a decision

1. *Du Pape*. [The work was originally published in 1820; see *Oeuvres Complètes de J. de Maistre*, vol. 2 (Lyon and Paris, 1928), chap. 1.—tr.]

is more important than how a decision is made. "It is definitely not in our interest that a question be decided in one way or another but that it be decided without delay and without appeal." In practice, not to be subject to error and not to be accused of error were for him the same. The important point was that no higher authority could review the decision.

Just as revolutionary radicalism was far more profound and consequential in the proletarian revolution of 1848 than in the 1789 revolution of the third estate, the intensity of the decision was also heightened in the political philosophy of the counterrevolution. Only by recognizing that trend can we understand the development from de Maistre to Donoso Cortés—from legitimacy to dictatorship. That radical heightening manifested itself in the increasing significance of the axiomatic theses on the nature of man. Every political idea in one way or another takes a position on the "nature" of man and presupposes that he is either "by nature good" or "by nature evil." This issue can only be clouded by pedagogic or economic explanations, but not evaded. For the rationalism of the Enlightenment, man was by nature ignorant and rough, but educable. It was thus on pedagogic grounds that the ideal of a "legal despotism" was justified: Uneducated humanity is educated by a legislator (who, according to Rousseau's *Social Contract*, was able "to change the nature of man"); or unruly nature could be conquered by Fichte's "tyrant," and the state became, as Fichte said with naive brutality, an "educational factory." Marxist socialism considers the question of the nature of man incidental and superfluous because it believes that changes in economic and social conditions change man. To the committed atheistic anarchists, man is decisively good, and all evil is the result of theological thought and its derivatives, including all ideas concerning authority, state, and government. In the *Social Contract*, with whose constructions in terms of the theory of the state de Maistre and Bonald were primarily concerned, man was by no means conceived to be by nature good; as Ernest Seillière has so splendidly demonstrated, only Rousseau's later novels unfolded the celebrated Rousseauian thesis of the good man. Donoso Cortés, in contrast, opposed Proudhon, whose antitheological anarchism would have to be derived consistently from the axiom of the good man, whereas the starting point for the Catholic Spaniard was the dogma of Original Sin. But Donoso Cortés radicalized this polemically into a doctrine of the absolute sinfulness and depravity of human nature. The dogma of Original Sin promulgated by the Council of Trent is not radical in any simple way. In contrast to the Lutheran understanding, the dogma asserts not absolute worthlessness but only distortion, opacity, or injury and leaves open the possibility of the natural good. Abbé Gaduel, who criticized Donoso Cortés from the standpoint of dogma, was therefore right when he voiced misgivings about his exaggeration of the natural evil and unworthiness of man. Yet it was certainly not right to have overlooked the fact that for Donoso Cortés this was a religious and political decision of colossal actuality, and not just the elaboration of dogma. When he spoke of the natural evil of man, he polemicized against atheist anarchism and its axiom of the good man; he meant ἀγωνικῶς and not δογματικῶς. Even though it appears that he agreed here with Lutheran dogma, his position was different from the Lutheran, which mandated obedience to every authority; he thus retained the self-confident grandeur of a spiritual descendant of the Grand Inquisitors.

What Donoso Cortés had to say about the natural depravity and vileness of man was indeed more horrible than anything that had ever been alleged by an absolutist philosophy of the state in justifying authoritarian rule. De Maistre too was capable of being shocked by the wickedness of man. His utterances on the nature of man gained force from his lack of illusions about morals and from solitary psychological experiences. Bonald was no less clear about the fundamentally evil instinct of man and recognized the indestructible "will to power," as do modern psychologists. But his conception of human nature pales in comparison to the outbursts of Donoso Cortés, whose contempt for man knew no limits: Man's blind reason, his weak will, and the ridiculous vitality of his carnal longings appeared to him so pitiable that all words in every human language do not suffice to express the complete lowness of this creature. Had God not become man, the reptile that my foot tramples would have been less contemptuous than a human being: "El reptil que piso con mis piés, seria á mis ojos menos despreciable que el hombre." The stupidity of the masses was just as apparent to him as was the silly vanity of their leaders. His awareness of sin was universal; he was even more horrified than a Puritan. No Russian anarchist in asserting that "man is good" expressed a greater degree of elementary conviction than the Spanish Catholic who said: Since God has not said it to him, whence does he know that he is good? "De donde sabe que es noble si Dios se lo ha dicho?" The despair of this man, as can be gathered from his letters to his friend Count Raczyński, often bordered on insanity; according to his philosophy of history, the victory of evil is self-evident and natural, and only a miracle by God can avert it. The pictures in which his impressions of human history were objectified were

full of dread and horror: Humanity reels blindly through a lab-
yrinth that we call history, whose entrance, exit, and shape nobody
knows;[2] humanity is a boat aimlessly tossed about on the sea
and manned by a mutinous, vulgar, forcibly recruited crew that
howls and dances until God's rage pushes the rebellious rabble
into the sea so that quiet can prevail once more.[3] But the typical
picture is a different one: the bloody decisive battle that has
flared up today between Catholicism and atheist socialism.

According to Donoso Cortés, it was characteristic of bourgeois
liberalism not to decide in this battle but instead to begin a
discussion. He straightforwardly defined the bourgeoisie as a
"discussing class," *una clasa discutidora.* It has thus been sentenced.
This definition contains the class characteristic of wanting to
evade the decision. A class that shifts all political activity onto
the plane of conversation in the press and in parliament is no
match for social conflict. The insecurity and immaturity of the
liberal bourgeoisie of the July Monarchy can be recognized everywhere. Its liberal constitutionalism attempted to paralyze the king
through parliament but permitted him to remain on the throne,
an inconsistency committed by deism when it excluded God from
the world but held onto his existence (here Donoso Cortés adopted
from Bonald the immensely fruitful parallel of metaphysics and
the theory of the state). Although the liberal bourgeoisie wanted
a god, its god could not become active; it wanted a monarch,
but he had to be powerless; it demanded freedom and equality
but limited voting rights to the propertied classes in order to
ensure the influence of education and property on legislation, as
if education and property entitled that class to repress the poor

---

2. *Obras de Don Juan Donoso Cortés,* vol. 5 (Madrid, 1855), p. 192.
3. *Obras de Don Juan Donoso Cortés,* vol. 4 (Madrid, 1854), p. 102.

and uneducated; it abolished the aristocracy of blood and family but permitted the impudent rule of the moneyed aristocracy, the most ignorant and the most ordinary form of an aristocracy; it wanted neither the sovereignty of the king nor that of the people. What did it actually want?

The curious contradictions of this liberalism struck not only reactionaries such as Donoso Cortés and F. J. Stahl but also revolutionaries such as Marx and Engels. Moreover we find a rare situation in which we can confront, in a concrete political context for once, a bourgeois German scholar of Hegelian education with a Spanish Catholic. Without influencing one another, both diagnose the same inconsistencies but offer different evaluations; thus they provide a contrast of the highest typological clarity. In his *Geschichte der sozialen Bewegung in Frankreich* Lorenz von Stein spoke in detail about the liberals: They wanted a monarch, in other words a supreme personal authority, with an independent will and independent action. Yet they made the king a mere executive organ with his every act dependent on the consent of the cabinet, thus removing once again that personal element. They wanted a king who would be above parties, who would thus also have to be above the people's assembly; and simultaneously they insisted that the king could not do anything but execute the will of this people's assembly. They declared the person of the king to be inviolable but had him take an oath on the constitution, so that a violation of the constitution became possible but could not be pursued. "No human ingenuity," said Stein, "is sufficiently sharp to resolve this contradiction conceptually." This must be doubly peculiar to a party such as the liberal, which after all prides itself on its rationalism. F.J. Stahl, a Prussian conservative, who in his lectures "Über die gegen-

wärtigen Parteien in Staat und Kirche" treated the many contradictions of constitutional liberalism, offered a very simple explanation: The hatred of monarchy and aristocracy drove the
liberal bourgeois leftward; the fear of being dispossessed of his
property, which was threatened by radical democracy and socialism, drove him in turn toward the right, to a powerful monarchy whose military could protect him. He thus oscillated
between his two enemies and wanted to fool both. Stein's explanation was entirely different. He replied by referring to "life"
and precisely attributed the many contradictions to the complexity
of life. The "irreconcilable merging of opposites into one another"
is "precisely the true character of all living things." Everything
that exists contains the opposite: "Pulsating life consists in the
continuous penetration of opposite forces, and in actuality they
are really opposites only when cut away from life." He then
compared the mutual penetration of opposites with what happens
in organic nature and in personal life, and then said of the state
that it too has a personal life. It belongs to the essence of life to
generate, slowly and constantly from within, new opposites, new
harmonies, and so on.

De Maistre and Donoso Cortés were incapable of such "organic" thinking. De Maistre showed this by his total lack of
understanding of Schelling's philosophy of life; Donoso Cortés
was gripped by horror when he was confronted with Hegelianism
in Berlin in 1849. Both were diplomats and politicians with much
experience and practice and had concluded sufficiently sensible
compromises. But a systematic and metaphysical compromise
was to them inconceivable. To suspend the decision at the crucial
point by denying that there was at all something to be decided
upon must have appeared to them to be a strange pantheistic

confusion. Liberalism, with its contradictions and compromises, existed for Donoso Cortés only in that short interim period in which it was possible to answer the question "Christ or Barabbas?" with a proposal to adjourn or appoint a commission of investigation. Such a position was not accidental but was based on liberal metaphysics. The bourgeoisie is the class committed to freedom of speech and freedom of the press, and it did not arrive at those freedoms from any kind of arbitrary psychological and economic conditions, from thinking in terms of trade, or the like. It has long been known that the idea of the liberal rights of man stemmed from the North American states. Though Georg Jellinek recently demonstrated the North American origin of those freedoms, the thesis would hardly have surprised the Catholic philosopher of the state (nor, incidentally, would it have surprised Karl Marx, the author of the essay on the Jewish question). Further, the economic postulates of free trade and commerce are, for an examination within the realm of the history of ideas, only derivatives of a metaphysical core. Donoso Cortés in his radical intellectuality saw only the theology of the foe. He did not "theologize" in the least; there were no ambiguous, mystical combinations and analogies, no Orphic oracle. The letters about actual political questions revealed a sober attitude, often frightening and without any sort of illusion or any touch of the quixotic; in his systematic train of thought there was an effort to be concise in the good dogmatic tradition of theology. His intuition into things intellectual was therefore often striking. His definition of the bourgeoisie as a *clasa discutidora* and his recognition that its religion resides in freedom of speech and of the press are examples. I do not consider this to be the last word on Continental liberalism in its entirety, but it is certainly a most striking observation. In view of the system of a Condorcet, for example, whose typical meaning Wolzendorff, perhaps because of intellectual affinity, recognized and superbly described, one must truly believe that the ideal of political life consists in discussing, not only in the legislative body but also among the entire population, if human society will transform itself into a monstrous club, and if truth will emerge automatically through voting. Donoso Cortés considered continuous discussion a method of circumventing responsibility and of ascribing to freedom of speech and of the press an excessive importance that in the final analysis permits the decision to be evaded. Just as liberalism discusses and negotiates every political detail, so it also wants to dissolve metaphysical truth in a discussion. The essence of liberalism is negotiation, a cautious half measure, in the hope that the definitive dispute, the decisive bloody battle, can be transformed into a parliamentary debate and permit the decision to be suspended forever in an everlasting discussion.

Dictatorship is the opposite of discussion. It belongs to the decisionism of one like Donoso Cortés to assume the extreme case, to anticipate the Last Judgment. That extremist cast of mind explains why he was contemptuous of the liberals while he respected atheist-anarchist socialism as his deadly foe and endowed it with a diabolical stature. In Proudhon he claimed to see a demon. Proudhon laughed about it, and alluding to the Inquisition as if he were already on the funeral pyre, he called out to Donoso Cortés: Ignite it![4] The satanism of that period was not an incidental paradox but a powerful intellectual principle. Its literary expression was the elevation of the throne of Satan—

4. An addition to the later editions of *Les confessions d'un Revolutionnaire*. [The first edition appeared in Paris in 1849. Later editions appeared in 1876 and 1929.—tr.]

the "adopted father of those who, in a fit of anger, cast out God the father from the earthly paradise"—and of Cain, the fratricide, while Abel, the bourgeois, was "warming his belly at the patriarchal hearthside." "The descendants of Cain ascend to heaven/ and on earth throw down God!" (Baudelaire).

But that position was untenable, primarily because it provided only for an exchange of roles on the part of God and the devil. Moreover, in comparison with later anarchists, Proudhon was a moralistic petit bourgeois who continued to subscribe to the authority of the father and the principle of the monogamous family. Bakunin was the first to give the struggle against theology the complete consistency of an absolute naturalism. Indeed he too wanted to "disseminate Satan," and this he considered the sole true revolution, in contrast to Karl Marx, who scorned every form of religion. Bakunin's intellectual significance rests, nevertheless, on his conception of life, which on the basis of its natural rightness produces the correct forms by itself from itself. For him, therefore, there was nothing negative and evil except the theological doctrine of God and sin, which stamps man as a villain in order to provide a pretext for domination and the hunger for power. All moral valuations lead to theology and to an authority that artificially imposes an alien or extrinsic "ought" on the natural and intrinsic truth and beauty of human life. The sources of such authority are greed and lust for power, and these result in a general corruption of those who exercise power as well as those over whom it is exercised. When anarchists today see in the patriarchal family and in monogamy the actual state of sin, and when they preach the return of matriarchy, the supposedly paradisiacal original state, they are manifesting a stronger awareness of the deepest connections than is reflected in Proudhon's laugh. Donoso Cortés always had in mind the final consequences of the dissolutions of the family resting on the authority of the father, because he saw that the moral vanished with the theological, the political idea with the moral, and all moral and political decisions are thus paralyzed in a paradisiacal worldliness of immediate natural life and unproblematic concreteness.

Today nothing is more modern than the onslaught against the political. American financiers, industrial technicians, Marxist socialists, and anarchic-syndicalist revolutionaries unite in demanding that the biased rule of politics over unbiased economic management be done away with. There must no longer be political problems, only organizational-technical and economic-sociological tasks. The kind of economic-technical thinking that prevails today is no longer capable of perceiving a political idea. The modern state seems to have actually become what Max Weber envisioned: a huge industrial plant. Political ideas are generally recognized only when groups can be identified that have a plausible economic interest in turning them to their advantage. Whereas, on the one hand, the political vanishes into the economic or technical-organizational, on the other hand the political dissolves into the everlasting discussion of cultural and philosophical-historical commonplaces, which, by aesthetic characterization, identify and accept an epoch as classical, romantic, or baroque. The core of the political idea, the exacting moral decision, is evaded in both. The true significance of those counterrevolutionary philosophers of the state lies precisely in the consistency with which they decide. They heightened the moment of the decision to such an extent that the notion of legitimacy, their starting point, was finally dissolved. As soon as Donoso

Cortés realized that the period of monarchy had come to an end because there no longer were kings and no one would have the courage to be king in any way other than by the will of the people, he brought his decisionism to its logical conclusion. He demanded a political dictatorship. In the cited remarks of de Maistre we can also see a reduction of the state to the moment of the decision, to a pure decision not based on reason and discussion and not justifying itself, that is, to an absolute decision created out of nothingness.

But this decisionism is essentially dictatorship, not legitimacy. Donoso Cortés was convinced that the moment of the last battle had arrived; in the face of radical evil the only solution is dictatorship, and the legitimist principle of succession becomes at such a moment empty dogmatism. Authority and anarchy could thus confront each other in absolute decisiveness and form a clear antithesis: De Maistre said that every government is necessarily absolute, and an anarchist says the same; but with the aid of his axiom of the good man and corrupt government, the latter draws the opposite practical conclusion, namely, that all governments must be opposed for the reason that every government is a dictatorship. Every claim of a decision must be evil for the anarchist, because the right emerges by itself if the immanence of life is not disturbed by such claims. This radical antithesis forces him of course to decide against the decision; and this results in the odd paradox whereby Bakunin, the greatest anarchist of the nineteenth century, had to become in theory the theologian of the antitheological and in practice the dictator of an antidictatorship.

Index